Self-Interest and Public Interest in Western Politics

COMPARATIVE EUROPEAN POLITICS

Comparative European Politics is a series for students and teachers of political science and related disciplines, published in association with the European Consortium for Political Research. Each volume will provide an up-to-date survey of the current state of knowledge and research on an issue of major significance in European government and politics.

OTHER TITLES IN THIS SERIES

Parties and Democracy: Coalition Formation and Government Functioning in Twenty States
Ian Budge and Hans Keman

Multiparty Government: The Politics of Coalition in Europe
Michael Laver and Norman Schofield

Government and Politics in Western Europe:
Britain, France, Italy, West Germany
Yves Mény

FORTHCOMING

Politics and Policy in the European Community (second edition)
Stephen George

Political Data Handbook: OECD Countries
Jan-Erik Lane, David McKay, and Kenneth Newton

Localism and Centralism in Europe:
The Political and Legal Bases of Local Self-Government
Edward Page

Self-Interest and Public Interest in Western Politics

LEIF LEWIN

Translated from the Swedish by
DONALD LAVERY

OXFORD UNIVERSITY PRESS
1991

Oxford University Press, Walton Street, Oxford OX2 6DP
Oxford New York Toronto
Delhi Bombay Calcutta Madras Karachi
Petaling Jaya Singapore Hong Kong Tokyo
Nairobi Dar es Salaam Cape Town
Melbourne Auckland
and associated companies in
Berlin Ibadan

Oxford is a trade mark of Oxford University Press

Published in the United States
by Oxford University Press, New York

British Library Cataloguing in Publication Data
Lewin, Leif 1941–
Self-interest and public interest in western politics. –
(Comparative European politics).
1. Western Europe. Politics
I. Title II. Series 320.94
ISBN 0–19–827726–1
ISBN 0–19–827725–3 (Pbk)

Library of Congress Cataloging in Publication Data
Lewin, Leif, 1941–
[Gemensamma bästa. English]
Self-interest and public interest in western politics / Leif Lewin;
translated from the Swedish by Donald Lavery.
p. cm. — (Comparative European politics)
Includes bibliographical references and index.
1. Public interest. 2. Common good. 3. Self-interest. 4. Social
choice. 5. Voting. I. Title. II. Series.
JC330.15.L4913 1991 320'.01'1—dc20 90–21502
ISBN 0–19–827726–1
ISBN 0–19–827725–3 (Pbk)

Typeset by Hope Services (Abingdon) Ltd.
Printed in Great Britain by Biddles Ltd.,
Guildford & King's Lynn

Contents

I

Self-Interest and Public Interest

Is it self-interest or public interest that predominates in public life? Does political man try primarily to fulfil personal desires and needs, or does he act with the intent to further what he believes to be best for society as a whole?

This is a question discussed by specialists in the fields of rational choice, political philosophy, and electoral research; however, since each field has adopted its own terminology and deals with these questions at different levels of abstraction, it cannot be said that there exists much dialogue between them. To establish cross-fertilization is the aim of this book. What is taken as a postulate for one field is dealt with as a problem in a second; what is deduced theoretically in one area is examined with empirical methods in some other; phenomena that are immediately elucidated with large amounts of data in one research tradition are subjected to thorough conceptual analysis in a second. Without letting on that their neighbour possesses the missing link in the chain of argument, the rational-choice theorists (or 'rationalists' for short), philosophers, and electoral researchers, with all too few exceptions, thus continue to talk at cross-purposes about how the common good can be achieved in politics.

'Doesn't one get the best explanation of the political game if one regards ideologies as mere beacons for selfish electors and billboards for vote-maximizing politicians?' wonder some rationalists, while others point to the difficulties in aggregating private preferences as rational, collective decisions. 'Is it really possible to distinguish the individual's self-interest from what he believes to be in the public interest?' wonder the philosophers. And the electoral researchers try to determine in their broad studies if the voters are mainly guided by private economic motives or by considerations more grounded on principle.

The aim of this study can be divided more precisely into three questions structured according to three different levels of the political system, all of which are dealt with, if in different ways, within each of the fields of research mentioned above:

1. Does the voter mainly follow the dictates of his pocket-book or some conception of the public interest?

2. Do politicians mainly strive to maximize their votes or to realize their electoral platform?

3. Do bureaucrats primarily try to maximize their budgets or to implement as loyal servants the political decisions of their masters?

Following this introductory chapter, in which the discourse of each of the three scientific fields is presented, the question whether the voter follows the dictates of his wallet is dealt with in Chapter 2, whether politicians are vote-maximizers in Chapter 3, and whether bureaucrats are budget-maximizers in Chapter 4. In the concluding chapter an explanation is offered of how the common good arises in politics.

The goal is thus theoretical and the main aim—once necessary conceptual distinctions have been made—to test empirically what, up to now, some scholars have mainly regarded as postulates (simply to be illustrated with hypothetical textbook examples) and what others have collected reams of information about (but seldom placed in a theoretical or philosophical context): namely the question of whether there exist any grounds for the assumption of the predominance of self-interest in Western politics. With such a design the results can always be criticized by the specialists in the various fields for not being sufficiently rigorous. But the purpose of the book is not primarily to make original contributions to specific discourses but rather to see how the same problem keeps emerging in different subdisciplines. This can make the book useful for both students and beginners who want a first contact with the problem and its classic literature. Scholars may also find it useful to reflect on the ways in which different theories and methods approach the same questions.

THE PROBLEM OF THE RATIONALISTS

During the 1950s and 1960s the scientific approach adopted in the natural sciences became the ideal among trend-setting social scientists.

With electoral studies taking the lead, human beings were treated as an object of research in principle like any other part of nature and the task of the researcher was to discover the general laws governing their behaviour. Towards the end of the 1960s this conception of science was faced with two simultaneous challenges: politically, in that the student revolts reacted against the attempts of electoral researchers to depreciate the importance of participation as a democratic norm, and scientifically, in that the rational-choice school emphasized the uniqueness of man since he is equipped with reason and a will of his own and is in no way subjected in his actions to a predetermined order.

'Rational choice' appears in two variants: 'public choice' and 'social choice'. What characterizes the former is the assumption that human beings are primarily guided by self-interest. In a standard work it is declared right on the very first page that 'the basic behavioral postulate of public choice . . . is that man is an egoistic, rational, utility maximizer'.[1] Whenever the hypothesis of self-interest is made the object of scrutiny in this book, we thus take the public-choice school as our point of departure. 'Social choice' is concerned with the purely logical difficulties involved in aggregating individual preferences, whatever these may be, to form collective decisions that reflect what the people actually want.

Both forms of rational choice thus presume that humans are rational beings that set certain goals for themselves and can also use suitable means to reach them. This conception of man leads to a very definite view of how research in the social sciences should be designed. All scientific explanations require that events and phenomena be related to certain general statements. Such statements can in principle be derived in two different ways: empirically by observing regularity and theoretically through postulating regularity. Electoral studies— like proverbs and weather forecasts—were relegated by the rational-choice school to the former category. The latter, deductive method has as its most distinguishing characteristic the notion that there exists a *reason* for the regularity. It was therefore suggested that if one is to succeed in explaining political actions, one ought to study the reasons, motives, and preferences of the actors.

To illustrate this point, it was suggested, one might consider the tossing of a coin. If it were to come up heads nine times in a row, this would certainly be a regularity which, according to the empirical method, would justify the generalization that the coin comes up heads. However, if one deals with postulated regularity, there must be some reason for the regularity and in this case there is of course no such reason. The coin has no 'preferences' of either a human or divine nature. The fact that it comes up heads nine times in a row is simply the chance outcome of 1 in 512. Theoretically, the best prediction for the next toss is that the odds are even that it will come up tails or heads.

Human action, it was further argued, is determined by completely different conditions. A human being is guided by his motives. If we see a man walking north, there is no greater reason to suppose that he is going to continue northward than to turn south, west, or east. As soon as we find out his destination, however, we can make a more accurate prediction of the direction he will choose and explain that choice.

The rational-choice school found it bizarre that electoral researchers should have dismissed the voters' behaviour as irrational (although not as bizarre as a non-explanatory theory would have been). The rationalists did not think much of these conclusions. In a study of what the citizen took into consideration it was on the contrary quite possible to explain participation in political elections, for example. 'This analysis of a citizen's decision to vote demonstrates how an act that some regard as irrational and that others study with a seemingly endless series of empirical generalizations can be understood with a simple cost–benefit calculus.'[2] That human beings are rational actors who act on the basis of deliberate although not necessarily accurate calculations is thus the basic theoretical premiss of rational choice.

One of the pioneer works of the public-choice school is Anthony Downs's *An Economic Theory of Democracy*, which was published in 1957. In his consistently deductive analysis Downs assumes that people act rationally even in politics—and by rational he means selfish: 'Thus, whenever we speak of rational behavior, we always mean rational behavior directed primarily towards selfish ends.' Downs took a few ironic pokes at those scholars who assumed that governments attempted to maximize the welfare of their citizens rather than to consolidate their power. After all, that would mean that our politicians would be 'perfect altruists in so far as their productive actions are concerned. They alone, among all the men in society, have no private motives other than discharging their social function.' It was more realistic, he felt, to compare political parties with private businesses. 'Our main thesis is that parties in democratic politics are analogous to entrepreneurs in a profit-seeking economy. So as to attain their private ends, they formulate whatever policies they believe will gain the most votes, just as entrepreneurs produce whatever products they believe will gain the most profits for the same reason.' The rationality of the citizen—i.e. that citizens were presumed to vote in a fashion that would best satisfy their self-interest—was the first basic premiss necessary for this argument. The second was the rationality of the parties' actions, something which was defined in terms of their fundamental goal of vote-maximization: 'parties formulate policies in order to win elections, rather than win elections in order to formulate policies'. From these two premisses a rich theory of elections in democracies was developed and a number of hypotheses derived. These hypotheses should be regarded as the touchstone of the theory: 'theoretical models should be tested primarily by the accuracy of their predictions rather than by the reality of their assumptions'.[3]

A few years later appeared *The Calculus of Consent* by James Buchanan and Gordon Tullock, a study that soon became as renowned as Downs's. Like the latter, the authors found parallels between politics and economics. 'Our purpose in this book is to derive a preliminary theory of collective choice that is in some respects analogous to the orthodox economic theory of markets.' Like economics, politics is characterized by exchange between two or more individuals with the purpose of meeting everyone's self-interest. The relation between Robinson Crusoe and Friday was taken to illustrate this point: Crusoe was a skilful fisherman while Friday was better at climbing trees to get coconuts. Both gained by exchanging goods and services with each other. It is the same in politics, the authors maintained. Behind political decisions can be glimpsed rational, welfare-maximizing individuals who in interaction with others ultimately attempt to look after their own interests. The traditional conception of political science that the individual as a voter tried to liberate himself from his selfish interests in order to discover 'the common good' was described as naïve. The public interest was nothing more than the fact that as many as possible had their desires fulfilled and politics should in consequence be organized in such a way that this process was facilitated. The work of Buchanan and Tullock took the form of a committed defence of the politics of reciprocal exchange, of 'log-rolling' as a political technique—a pejorative term the authors wished to rehabilitate. Like Downs they were not interested in the behaviour of the political leaders or in their dealings with each other. Their point of view was that of the individual citizen and their method of research was strictly logical. They began with the assumption that individuals are rational and welfare-maximizers. 'First, on the basis of certain initial postulates and assumptions, the logical consequences can be developed. This sort of theorizing is purely logical in nature and has no empirical relevance in the direct sense. Herein, theory resembles mathematics.' From these they formulated—again, as did Downs—testable predictions that would be able to demonstrate the predictive value of the theory in practice.[4]

Thus voters and politicians were represented as rational, welfare-maximizing individuals concerned with their own self-interest. The third group of actors—the bureaucrats—soon came to be included in public-choice theory as well. Tullock claimed in *The Politics of Bureaucracy* (1965) that governmental agencies, in contradistinction to private enterprises, expand without any attempt at minimizing their costs.[5]

In *Inside Bureaucracy* (1967) Downs put forward an elaborated, deductive theory of how this bureaucratic growth could be explained with the hypothesis of self-interest. He contended that bureaucrats tried to improve their own welfare in terms of salary, esteem, and influence by seeing to it that their office became as large as possible. Aggressive budget demands and expansive reorganization were part of this deliberate endeavour. Even in the exercise of official duties the bureaucrat acted more from considerations of personal advantage than from loyalty to the intentions of the legislature.[6]

William Niskanen followed up the size argument in his elegant *Bureaucracy and Representative Government* (1971). The author suggested the term 'budget maximization' to describe the attitude of the administration to its allocated resources. In contrast to administrators in private enterprise, bureaucrats had neither the will nor the motivation to economize. On the contrary, they tried to increase their salaries and other benefits with larger budgets. Year after year their policy was to get an increase in their appropriations. All notions of marginal-cost analysis, which would counteract such expansion, were absent from their thinking, and the government therefore lacked counter-arguments when the bureaucrats demanded more resources for their operations. In this manner it came to be a characteristic of bureaucracies to be wasteful of national resources and to have unnecessarily large budgets.[7]

In these studies Downs, Buchanan, Tullock, and Niskanen all held consistently to the fundamental premiss that the motives of the individual are selfish. The objects of analysis were not individuals, however, but collective social phenomena such as the outcome of elections, the decisions of the legislature, and the activities of the public services. The individuals were merely tools of analysis; the point of the exercise was to account for collective decision-making. This way of going about the study followed from the extremely important principle of 'methodological individualism', which denied the possibility of deriving meta-individual values of principles directly from the collectivity—'holism', 'organic theory', 'paternalism', 'idealism', or whatever this approach might be called. Collective concepts such as 'the public interest', 'the common good', 'the will of the people', and 'the national interest' could only be determined, it was argued, through aggregating the preferences of the separate individuals.

It consequently became a task of central importance to examine which rules should guide such an aggregation. As mentioned above, this became the concern of that speciality within the rational-choice school which is usually called 'social choice'. The defects of the majority rule, the one most often applied in politics, were soon made apparent. The problems of intransitiveness and intensity within a democracy were revealed. The former is that the preferences of an individual need not be hierarchically ordered but can be circular. The latter is that citizens are generally more concerned about certain questions than about others although their influence does not vary for this reason, something pointed out by those who would like collective decisions to reflect the preferences of citizens but which is rejected by those who regard the principle of 'one man-one vote' as a political right independent of utilitarian concerns.

It was Kenneth Arrow who made the most penetrating study of this problem. In his classic work *Social Choice and Individual Values* (first published as early as 1951, the second, enlarged, edition in 1963), Arrow followed the path taken by the French philosopher of the Enlightenment, Condorcet, and demonstrated no decision-making rule exists that guarantees collective rationality even if each individual acts rationally in relation to his own preferences. Arrow laid down five simple conditions that he considered a decision-making rule should fulfil. In the first place, there should not be any limits on the way the citizens order their preferences. Secondly, there should exist a positive correlation between collective and individual preferences: the collective decision must remain unchanged or change in the same direction as a change in individual preferences; it must not change in the opposite direction. Thirdly, the decision should be independent of irrelevant alternatives: the collective decision must not change unless the individual preferences have changed. The final two conditions imply that preferences cannot be forced upon an actor from without ('citizen-sovereignty') or dictated by any single actor ('non-dictatorship'). The difficulty with these five conditions, which surely most people could agree to, is that their goals are incompatible. They cannot all be satisfied at the same time by any one decision-making rule.[8]

A similar idea is expressed in the well-known example of the 'prisoners' dilemma'. If both of two prisoners who are locked up in isolation cells without any opportunity of communicating with each other adopt the strategy that leads to their common good and deny that they have committed the crime of which they are jointly accused, they get off lightly with a two-year sentence for a smaller crime they are already proven guilty of. However, the punishments for the various combinations of strategies are so distributed that each prisoner has reason, both out of fear of a heavier twenty-year sentence if, despite his own plea of innocence, he were to be found guilty through the confession of the other prisoner and out of hope of getting a lighter one-year sentence as a reward for co-operating with the court, to adopt the strategy of confessing. But if both prisoners reason along these lines and confess, they are of course convicted of the crime of which they are accused and are sentenced to ten years' imprisonment, which is precisely what the judge, having boned up on game-theory, has so cleverly counted on the whole time. This is the way it is sometimes in politics as well. An important idea was thus introduced: rational action on the part of each individual need not lead to a rational outcome for all.

Following these studies there has occurred a veritable explosion of books on rationalistic explanation—both by 'public choice' with its hypothesis of self-interest and by 'social choice' with its concern for the problem of aggregation. It is no superficial or glossy image of a problem-free world dominated by rational actors that is depicted in these works, a charge initially laid against the school on account of its assumption of human rationality and free will. On the contrary, the rationalists demonstrate the fundamental contradiction that can exist between the preferences of private individuals and the common good. In their political roles as voters, elected representatives, or bureaucrats, human beings are also guided by private motives that can militate against the public interest. Even the best of intentions can go wrong because of the inner logic of the context of action; collective decisions can be taken that do not correspond to the first choice of any of the actors involved.

If one attempts to trace rationalistic explanation back through the history of ideas, one finds that it appears to be part of the heritage of utilitarianism and its two underlying assumptions:(*a*) what is best for society is nothing other than the sum of what is best for its individual members and (*b*) each person is the best judge of his own best interests. It is not only the spirit of Condorcet but also that of Smith, Mill, and Bentham that hovers over the theory.[9]

Placed in such a broad perspective, the contribution of rationalistic explanation—to put it succinctly—can be said to consist in having shown on purely theoretical grounds that the first assumption of utilitarianism is not valid. What is best for society is often not at all the same thing as the sum of what is best for the individuals; if the private person only considers his own selfish interests, society may suffer. There consequently seems to be a need once again to redirect research in the social sciences. 'Methodological individualism' should be supplemented with research directly aimed at those phenomena which occur between the individual person and law making—statutes, parties, organizations, the civil service. 'Organization of political life makes a difference.'[10] Often the purpose of these institutions, *pace* the utilitarians, is not to depart from but to counteract the expressed preferences of individuals. It is indeed to provide for the interests of the whole that decision-makers oft-times go against individual preferences when these are seen simply to be selfish special interests. The conclusion to be drawn from this could very well be the direct opposite to that maintained by the public-choice school in a political connection: the image of human beings as rational utility-maximizing individuals was thought to minimize the need for collective decision-making functions but the demonstrated difficulties involved in furthering the common good simply through the action of individuals points rather to the need to strengthen the public interest inasmuch as it is partly independent of individual preferences.

THE PROBLEM OF THE PHILOSOPHERS

To step from the discourse of the rationalists to that of the philosophers is to remove oneself from a world of daring postulates and imaginative theories to reflection's quieter retreat, more suited to the demons of doubt and objection. In their arguments the philosophers are generally as happily unconcerned with empirical evidence as the rationalists. They devote their attention however to an explication of the two fundamental concepts of how it is at all possible to know what a person's interest is and how the meaning of the notion of general interest is to be determined.

To begin with self-interest, the philosophers point out at least five difficulties, all of which are logically interconnected with each other.

In the first place, Amartya Sen maintains, it is not possible to derive a person's self-interest from his *behaviour*. After all, this is influenced by a great number of other conditions, some of which are social in character. How would it be, for example, if one were to suppose that a person's self-interest was revealed in the choices made? In the 'prisoners' dilemma' one would be obliged to conclude that the prisoners themselves wished to be sentenced to ten years' imprisonment. No, outward behaviour is a treacherous source of knowledge of a person's interests. The scholar must try to discover what it is the actor wills in his heart of hearts.[11]

However, it is no simple matter to determine a person's *will* either. Let us take the use of seat-belts as an example since that is a question that greatly interests the philosophers. Despite the fact that a person knows that the use of a seat-belt reduces injuries in a collision and that he has greater 'negative utility', as the rationalists say, from a traffic injury than from the very slight inconvenience of wearing a seat-belt, it does happen that the person in question refrains from using his seat-belt. The philosophers call this 'weakness of the will'. Through various forms of so-called self-binding it is possible to compensate for such weakness: the politician makes a public promise not to adopt a certain course of action; the bourgeois wife asks a lady-friend to attend a meeting she has with the man she has fallen in love with in order to eliminate the possibility of her betraying her marriage vows. Sometimes people do not really know what they want, writes Albert Weale, quite simply because they have inconsistent desires: a person who wants to stop smoking nevertheless longs for a cigarette. Weale's utopian 'alternative to utilitarianism' is a society that makes it difficult for its citizens to succumb to such temporary weakness of the will.[12]

The problem of weakness of the will makes it difficult to interpret particular expressions of the will. Does that person not get any enjoyment out of going to a café or does he refrain from doing so because he has resolved to lose weight? Is what confronts us when we observe a person a genuine manifestation of that person's will or merely a strategy to compensate for weakness of the will?

To investigate behaviour as expressions of will when one studies animals can probably be justified, Sen writes, since direct communication is in this case excluded (unless one is Dr Dolittle). But when it comes to human beings one should ask how they motivate their actions.[13]

When one studies *motivations*, however, one can easily jump from the frying-pan into the fire. If one believes that self-interest is to be found in expressed motivations, one is liable never to find anything for it is in terms of public interest, not self-interest, that people try to justify their positions. When textile-workers demand tariff protection, they do not support this by referring to the wages they expect but rather to the consequences unchecked competition from low-wage countries could have, in their estimation, for the economy of the country as a whole. This is the reason, writes Brian Barry in summarizing the large amount of literature inspired by the work of Arthur Bentley and David Truman, that many maintain that the primary function of the public interest is 'merely that of casting an aura of legitimacy around decisions which are in fact the outcome of group pressures'. To determine a person's true self-interest one must go behind the rhetorical motivations, which are intended to persuade and convince, and get at the actual assessments the person makes of what lies in his interest.[14]

But not even such *assessments* can always be trusted. When a person expresses the opinion that 'this is in my interest' or 'this is what I want to do', there is in many instances, perhaps most, no reason to question such a statement. In all essentials, the philosophers lend their support to the rationalists' view of man as an actor who knows which goals he holds and which means will be used to achieve them. Sometimes, however, expressed assessments lack credibility. What happens, for example, if the goal a person sets himself turns out to be unreachable? Resignation is of course one possibility. But one can also imagine other perhaps more likely psychological reactions on the part of the actor, reactions that are related to weakness of the will. The person in question may for example persuade himself that the goal he cannot achieve is not really worth the trouble. As Jon Elster so vividly points out, the person acts like the fox in the fable who declares the grapes to be sour.[15] But of course such self-deceit cannot be accepted if one truly wishes to find out what a person's interest is.

Thus none of the indirect methods discussed above guarantees that one gets at a person's self-interest. Neither through the observation of a person's behaviour, manifestations of will, motivations, or assessments can one be certain of discovering what a person actually wants. The only thing that finally remains is to go directly to the person's expressed preferences. However, even this does not guarantee that true interest will be found, for an actor can after all be mistaken about his preferences. 'He misjudges his "real" preferences', writes Felix Oppenheim, 'e.g., he runs after wealth when health is actually more valuable to him. An actor's real preferences may thus differ from those he believes he has . . . Everybody is not always the best judge of his best interests.'[16]

This is a fundamental point in the discussion of the philosophers,[17] one that was already recognized by John Stuart Mill and that has since his time given rise to an intense debate on the ruler's right—others say outright duty—to depart from the citizens' expressed preferences for their own good without thereby falling into odious paternalism.[18]

The admission that the private individual sometimes can be wrong about his own preferences has far-reaching consequences; indeed, it can be said to constitute a second telling blow against utilitarianism. If pointing out the problem of collective irrationality undermines the first premiss of utilitarianism, namely that what is best for society is the sum of what is best for its individual members, the second premiss that each man is the best judge of his own interests is found to be failing by this fact that the individual sometimes is mistaken concerning his own true interests.

Matters are not made any easier when the philosophers turn from the analysis of how self-interest is to be ascertained to a discussion of the meaning of public interest. The notion that the latter may arise through an aggregation of the private interests of the various citizens is one the rationalists themselves have largely helped disprove, as noted above. Through other types of arguments the philosophers arrive at a similar conclusion. Even if one knew what self-interest is, something the philosophers are in general not prepared to accept, it is very unclear how one is to go about aggregating interests. Their discussion of public interest can be reconstructed along a sliding scale on which, step by step, the various scholars remove themselves ever further from the atomistic argument of utilitarianism whereby the unseen hand arranges everything for the best of the whole. The majority of philosophers have difficulty seeing how the public interest can be satisfied without being influenced by a higher-order notion of what is best for the whole.

When people attempt to determine what is in the public interest, as opposed to self-interest, many of them naturally think spontaneously that it is a question of widening their horizons beyond their *personal preferences*. They try to take into consideration the needs and wishes of their fellows as well. But in doing so they make a blunder that could be called double counting, writes Ronald Dworkin, who does not believe there to be any need of a meta-level notion of 'the whole'. He clarifies his point by taking the example of a local government that is faced with the choice of building a swimming-pool or a theatre. Now there may well be local citizens who prefer the swimming-pool even if they themselves are unable to swim: they may admire some swimmer or they believe that theatre is sinful—or perhaps they share both of these views. If the 'external' preferences of these people are counted, the personal preferences of the swimmers are reinforced and

the result will be a form of double counting: each swimmer will have the benefit not only of his own preference, but also of the preference of someone else who takes pleasure in his success. If the moralistic preferences are counted, the effect will be the same: actors and audiences will suffer because their preferences are held in lower respect by citizens whose personal preferences are not themselves engaged.

If one wishes to understand utilitarianism correctly and insist upon political equality amongst citizens, only personal preferences should therefore be counted when the public interest is determined. Such is Dworkin's paradoxical but straightforward argument.[19]

He is almost alone in reducing the argument to such an absurdity, however. The main line of argument in the philosophical discussion adopts the more intuitive understanding of the notion of public interest as something broader, something that takes into consideration not only selfish interests but also the needs of others. From a practical point of view, writes Peter Hammond, the problem of aggregation in determining the public interest boils down to the fact that the interests of some people conflict with the interests of others. The solution might therefore lie in including only *compatible preferences*. A land-owner may for example be considered to have the right to cut down all his trees, but if all landowners were to do the same, a risk of soil erosion would arise. Utilitarianism must consequently be modified to the extent that the community sets limits on which interests are to be included in the summing up. No particular interest should be pursued so far that it infringes upon another.[20]

John Harsanyi goes a further step closer to paternalism. Like Dworkin, he distinguishes between personal and external preferences (but calls them respectively 'subjective' and 'ethical' instead). His recommendation is however the direct opposite of Dworkin's: only the latter, the *ethical preferences*, should be aggregated. Harsanyi does not even hesitate to 'exclude', as he puts it, any personal preferences he finds 'irrational' or 'antisocial'. As originally formulated, utilitarianism stood in conflict to the traditional morality, according to Harsanyi. Take the act of promising as an example. For a utilitarian it is only the outcome of each action that counts. To break a promise is consequently acceptable if it leads to greater good for the whole. But what sort of a society would we have with such a morality? One should rather distinguish between what Harsanyi calls 'act utilitarianism' and 'rule utilitarianism'. The former entails that the criterion of utility is directly applied to an action: that line of action which maximizes utility is the one that should be followed. 'Rule utilitarianism' on the other hand prescribes that the utility criterion is not applied to particular actions but rather to the fundamental principles that govern these actions. According to this point of view, the right action is the one that conforms with moral laws and these moral laws should in turn be such that they would yield the greatest good for society if they were followed by all. According to Harsanyi only 'rule utilitarianism' can defend itself against the charge of advocating a Machiavellian morality.

No matter how sympathetic the reader might be to such an argument, he cannot avoid wondering how far one can reasonably go in reinterpreting a doctrine without changing its original name. In the end, Harsanyi's treatment of the problems of utilitarianism leads him to hold a sort of Kantian moral philosophy.[21]

On this point Amartya Sen expresses himself with his usual exemplary clarity. He draws Harsanyi's views on 'rule utilitarianism' to their logical conclusion and says quite simply that the best approximation of the public interest can be had not from the actors' preferences but from their *convictions*. Two boys find two apples, one large and one small. 'You choose', says the first boy, whereupon the second takes the larger apple. This upsets the first boy. 'Why?' wonders the second. 'Which one would *you* have chosen?' 'The smaller one, of course.' 'Then what are you complaining about?' the second boy retorts triumphantly. 'That's the one you've got!' Admittedly, he wins the argument (and the larger apple) but he does so by breaking certain rules of decency. Sen contends that the social sciences make the same mistake when they describe all human beings as full-blooded egoists who on every occasion strive to win as great an advantage as possible. On the contrary, he says, people are guided by their convictions about which values should be protected and fostered in society.

The basic norm of utilitarianism, that each individual should act so as to achieve the greatest total good, implies after all that sometimes, perhaps indeed quite often, one is obliged to refrain from what is best for oneself. Utilitarianism might therefore be criticized, not because it encourages egoism, but on the contrary because it demands too much of individuals in requiring that they sacrifice themselves to increase the total utility.

To allow that people are guided by convictions could have far-reaching ramifications. Much depends of course on how the concept of rationality is defined. If one imagines action to be consistent, there is no reason to suppose that the assumption that people act on their convictions need entail any major changes in the theory. On the other hand, it would no longer be possible to maintain the position that each action can be explained by selfish motives or that the citizen assesses actions exclusively in terms of their consequences in each particular case and solely as far as they affect him personally. Moreover, a calculus so narrow that it does not allow one to refrain from personal advantage out of consideration of others would leave unexplained why it is that people sometimes forgo a pleasure of the moment for a future one or why they bother at all to judge long-term and general effects. To suppose that human beings are guided by their convictions is more realistic than to depict them as rational fools—to use Sen's telling expression.[22]

At this point we can state that we have come round to the position diametrically opposite to utilitarianism: we have ended up with the morality of convictions that belongs to paternalism. The individual does not always understand what lies in his best interest. What is best for society is not the sum of individual interests. It can only be understood if each and every person, without allowing himself to be distracted by private advantage or the particular interests of others, quietly thinks out what is best for the community as a whole. Or as Walter Lippmann has expressed it: 'I suggest, that the public interest may be presumed to be what men would choose if they saw clearly, thought rationally, acted disinterestedly and benevolently.'[23]

Does this philosophy of the Age of the Enlightenment stand in conflict with the democratic notion that decisions must spring from the preferences of the citizens, that power is founded in the people? Does this mean that Burke with his philosophy of representation and the old paternalists win the game in the end?

No, not necessarily. The solution lies in fact close at hand. In contrast to the leaders of Victorian society, those who hold power today must submit to the test of election through general and equal suffrage, such that the interests of all citizens make themselves felt with the same weight. This democratic procedure is considered by certain authors to be the very quintessence of the common good: if the concept of public interest is difficult to define, the manner in which it is exercised through elected representatives becomes all the more important. 'The public-interest concept makes no operational sense', Glendon Schubert writes. But the democratic process itself can constitute a good substitute. By itself, this process does not guarantee that the public interest is always observed. But it leads to open decisions in which consideration is taken of all relevant interests and points of view and thus to the best possible approximation to the public interest. 'Decisions that are the product of a process of full consideration are most likely to be decisions in the public interest.'[24]

Thus is procedure substituted for content. The public interest is given an operational definition. What is in the public interest is made equivalent to what the elected representatives of the people declare it to be.

THE PROBLEM OF THE ELECTORAL RESEARCHERS

The subtle hints on the part of the philosophers that the electoral researchers belong to a less-sophisticated breed who print their questionnaires and set off on their investigations without devoting the matter much thought are, for the most part, grossly unfair. The contribution of the electoral researchers is, however, of a sort different from that of the rationalists or the philosophers. While the latter make matters easier for themselves by erecting purely abstract models or tying their reflections to fictive examples about the problems of the individual, the electoral researchers set themselves the immensely more difficult task of finding out what causes the actual behaviour of a whole nation of people. While the rationalists postulate that self-interest is the main cause and the philosophers point out the difficulties involved in defining this concept, the electoral researchers test empirically—amongst many other things—whether it is self-interest or public interest that primarily determines the way citizens vote. Their research has thereby stimulated the development of techniques for data collection, analysis, and conceptual reconstruction that are among the most advanced in the social sciences.

Electoral research springs from the breakthrough for democracy in several European countries towards the end of the First World War. When the political system was changed through the introduction of universal and equal suffrage, it was quite natural that political science should gain a new subdiscipline. Political scientists began to investigate systematically the forms of expression, causes, and consequences of political behaviour.[25]

To put it briefly, the methodological problems of the electoral researchers lie in the secret ballot. While this constitutes an irrevocable condition for democracy, it entails considerable difficulties from the point of view of the researcher. The task of the electoral researchers can be said to consist in revealing what underlies the anonymous result and in identifying those groups that support the political parties.

In principle, there are two ways of solving this problem; they have given rise to the two research traditions that have dominated electoral research. The older, for the most part European, method draws conclusions from observations of the correlation between social and political structures. Even if one does not know how the individuals have voted, one can in most countries get a hold of election data at a higher level of aggregation: the election results for districts, municipalities, and counties are known. From other sources one can obtain information about the social conditions in the same geographic areas and after that one can try to assess the connection between the areas' socio-cultural characteristics and their voting profile. Amongst studies that have been carried out along these lines may be mentioned André Siegfried's pioneering study *Tableau politique de la France de l'Ouest sous la Troisième République*, Herbert Tingsten's *Political Behavior*, and Rudolf Herberle's *From Democracy to Nazism*.[26]

Finding comparable data for such calculations has not always been a simple matter. Nor have the attempts at constructing a model to show how the widely disparate social phenomena that have interested researchers are related to each other and to the dependent variable (voting) always been successful. Nevertheless, the crucial difficulty with this so-called aggregate analysis is the statistical technique itself, for it has been shown that the correlations found at the aggregate level in many cases are not significant at the level of the individual and it is ultimately the political behaviour of the private individual we wish to understand. As a result of a famous article in 1950 on this ecological fallacy, as it is called, aggregate analysis more or less ceased to exist for a long time as a research approach.[27]

As luck would have it, by this time the second method of conducting electoral research had already begun. This younger, originally American, tradition entails that one interviews a representative sample of the population one wishes to study. This is of course the most radical solution to the methodological problem created by the secret ballot. Survey researchers, as they are called, quite simply ask citizens to tell them how they voted and also to inform them about other social and psychological characteristics of interest for a comparison with voting.

Even if some interview studies were made as early as the 1920s,[28] the real breakthrough for this method of analysis did not come until near the end of the Second World War when Lazarsfeld, Berelson, and Gaudet published *The People's Choice*. There soon followed a number of studies that attracted considerable attention: e.g. the sequel *Voting* (1954), and the Michigan group's *The Voter Decides* (1954), and *The American Voter* (1960). Electoral studies became established around the world. In Western Europe, as in the United States, political scientists regularly conduct studies in connection with national elections.[29]

During the 1950s and 1960s electoral research was dominated by the survey method. After that, however, there followed a third period characterized by renewed interest in aggregate analysis, at the same time as survey research was pushed further with unabated energy. It was the computer that gave researchers new hope of being able to overcome the problems associated with the enormous amounts of data required by aggregate analysis and the intricacies of the ecological fallacy. A fruitful collaboration between the two traditions in electoral research was begun. Survey researchers began to make 'ecologically corrected samples' of the people to be interviewed in order to capture the regional difference that might be found in the voting behaviour of various occupational categories. The researchers using aggregate data began to interpret their results with the help of the fine-tuned insights into political behaviour that had been revealed by survey research. It cannot be said any longer that there is a methodological struggle between the two, if indeed there ever was one.

It is self-evident to serious investigators of both breeds that neither data source taken alone is entirely satisfying. There are many exciting questions to be approached through aggregate data that can be confronted only ineffectively, if at all, with survey materials. And conversely, there are questions deftly answered by survey information that aggregated data comment upon only after a frightening series of inferential leaps or leave as a nest of complete indeterminacy. Thus, between them, the two types of data open up to us an extent of ground that neither taken alone would permit us to cover.[30]

Regarding our question of whether it is self-interest or public interest that is most prevalent in politics, an intense methodological debate has also been carried on between proponents of aggregate and survey techniques concerning the best way of finding an answer. A more detailed presentation of this discussion is given in the next chapter.

Right from their first studies the survey researchers painted a rather dismal picture of the public spirit of the average citizen and more generally of his ability to live up to the classical democratic ideals of the informed, rational, and disinterested voter. Paul Lazarsfeld had previously done research on consumer behaviour and expected that citizens, like consumers, would gather information without bias from different sources and then choose from the alternatives available. It turned out instead that the great majority of voters had made up their minds which party they would vote for long before the election campaign had even begun and that they received information in a selective fashion that only served to reinforce their original opinion. The model of the rational voter was replaced by an explanatory model inspired by natural science in which the voter was depicted as a socially determined being rather than one who chooses critically. It was difficult to imagine that the voter, frequently ignorant of or indifferent to politics and heavily' influenced by his own group's interests, could be guided by some conception of the public interest, wrote Bernard Berelson in the closing chapter of *Voting*:

The democratic citizen is supposed to cast his vote on the basis of principle— not fortuitously or frivolously or impulsively or habitually, but with reference

to standards not only of his own interest but of the common good as well . . .
Many voters vote not for principle in the usual sense but 'for' a group to which
they are attached—their group. The Catholic vote or the hereditary vote is
explainable less as principle than as a traditional social allegiance. The
ordinary voter, bewildered by the complexity of modern political problems,
unable to determine clearly what the consequences are of alternative lines of
action, remote from the arena, and incapable of bringing information to bear
on principle, votes the way trusted people around him are voting.[31]

But despite these shortcomings on the part of the individual voter,
the electoral researchers found that the democratic system nevertheless worked. Were our demands on the individual voter perhaps
unnecessarily high? Classical democratic doctrine now underwent a
'revision' according to which the supposed apathy and self-interest
of the citizen were not merely tolerated but were even declared to ·
perform a constructive function for the survival of democracy. It was
pointed out that strong interests and ideological commitment could
lead to intolerance and fanaticism that threatened democratic values.
The collapse of democracy in Europe in the inter-war period was
taken as a warning. In place of a high level of political participation on
the part of the citizens as the linchpin of democracy, the electoral
researchers emphasized the role of the political leaders. What gave
democracies their special character, it was maintained, was the fact
that they were not governed by one élite but by many and that these
leaders received their power through open competition for the votes of
the people.[32]

The defenders of the classical doctrine were not slow in replying,
however. 'Voters are not fools!' exclaimed V. O. Key.[33] A number of
researchers attempted to show both that the voters are actually guided
by reason and principle to a greater extent than electoral researchers
had tried to maintain and that the classical norms of participation and
public interest should be upheld in order to develop democracy
further, a point that quickly became widely accepted as a result of the
student revolts that flared up in the late 1960s.

More recent developments have led to a renewed interest in rational
models in electoral research as well. The focus of research has shifted
away from the social determinants of voting to the manner in which
opinions are formed at the moment of voting. At one end of the model
that electoral researchers work with is found the dependent variable
(voting behaviour) and at the other end various structural and historical

causes that influence the voter. Between these lie different social, psychological, and political factors that influence the private voter's deliberations.[34] Investigators have noted that opinion voting has increased and class voting has decreased in Western democracies. Citizens are becoming more and more independent of their social origins, vote more often on the basis of party platforms, and switch parties to an increasing extent as well. When all is said and done, is reality at least moving closer to the classical democratic ideal of the informed and rational voter who intends to further what he regards as the public interest?

Without trying to answer this question—as noted above, this will be the aim of the next chapter—a couple of reflections on the methodological issue could be made here. Is it really the case that opinion voting and class voting are incompatible phenomena? And is the latter obviously less rational than the former? According to class voting workers vote for a socialist party and the middle class for a non-socialist party. The blue-collar and white-collar worker may each have good reasons for their different choices, reasons that have nothing to do with group interests. It may be the considered opinion of the blue-collar worker that the welfare policies of the Social Democrats are best for the country as a whole, regardless of the fact that he himself will enjoy some of the benefits; the white-collar worker may similarly consider that the public interest is best served by deregulation and more elbow-room for market forces even if he does not personally stand to gain by the change. It is by no means certain that the electorate becomes more 'rational' if these two voters change their opinions and each votes for the other's previous party. Nor is it certain that a greater frequency of party switching is necessarily a sign of increasing rationality. It must of course be granted that there is a considerable amount of routine voting, where voters choose the same old party as last time without giving the matter much thought. Nevertheless, party loyalty may also be founded in one's experience that the party one usually votes for generally stands for a policy one approves of.

Yet another of the problems facing electoral researchers when they start to work with models of rational behaviour is that the dependent and independent variables tend to coincide with each other. The more one departs from the model of natural science and begins to take an interest in the opinions and motives of the voters, the greater the risk becomes of arriving at rather trivial conclusions. One scholar has noted ironically 'that the surest theory in electoral research seems to be that the voters tend to vote for the party they like best'.[35]

Those who investigate elections are thus still struggling with serious problems and any use of their results must be made with caution and critical judgement. However, it is only by using their data that we can find an answer to the question of whether it is self-interest or public interest that predominates amongst the electorate.

In this way might the problem of the rationalists, the philosophers, and the electoral researchers be summarized. The dividing line between them is naturally not as sharp as this sketch might suggest. Some scholars contribute to more than one field. Anthony Downs does not neglect to refer to electoral research from time to time when he believes that it supports his hypotheses. Amartya Sen discusses both the voting paradox of the rational-choice school and the concept of interest from a philosophical standpoint. And electoral researchers like Bernard Berelson are fond of concluding with a chapter in which they raise the broad philosophical questions of how the interest of the whole can be satisfied despite the self-interest and political apathy of the private citizen. One's main impression is none the less that political scientists have occupied themselves since the war in erecting a Tower of Babel. As research has become more specialized, the general view has become lost from sight. We still lack a comprehensive assessment of whether it is mainly self-interest or public interest that leaves its mark on the political process in the liberal countries of the West.

POINTS OF DEPARTURE

When one becomes aquainted with all these formidable methodological problems confronting the various research specialities, it is easy to feel that it would be a futile effort to try to find out what place is held by self-interest and public interest in politics. Is it the case, as some philosophers have resignedly concluded, that the only intellectually respectable position is that we can know nothing with certainty about these matters?

In spite of everything, it seems to be premature to draw such a conclusion, as feeble as it is irrefutable. The methodological debate certainly urges one to be extremely attentive so that one truly measures what one intends to examine. But to suppose that self-interest and public interest are ghost-like twins that vanish into thin air as soon as the researcher tries to get a grip on them appears to be an unreasonably pessimistic exaggeration. One of the starting-points for this study is instead the more constructive position formulated by such scholars as Brian Barry, Felix Oppenheim, and Roland Pennock. Barry objects to the fact that 'it has become fashionable in some quarters to dismiss the concept of "the public interest" as devoid of content'. He claims by contrast that both concepts are usable in research, that 'it makes good sense to suppose that there are interests common to all the members of a community', and that 'to say "x is in the public interest" has a fairly clear meaning and is by no means equivalent to nothing more precise that "I favour x"'.[36]

Quite contrary to the supposition that the concept of public interest cannot be used meaningfully, Oppenheim maintains 'that this notion, like that of self-interest, can be defined in descriptive terms and used independently of our own preferences'.[37]

According to Pennock, the fact that the notion of public interest is vague does not make it impossible to use. If one were to apply such a principle, our language would be made completely destitute. Take for example the expression 'a beautiful woman'. On this point every man considers himself an expert; since the beginning of time men have carried on a lively discussion about which characteristics are of particular importance in judging the beauty of women. Nevertheless, the upshot—at least within each culture—is usually a remarkable degree of agreement about which women should be placed in this category. No one would dream of defining a beautiful woman operationally as one who wins a beauty contest. Nor would anyone wish to deny that beautiful women exist. In fact, we can be reasonably certain of which physical attributes are possessed by women who are singled out as beautiful.

The same thing is true of the public interest, Pennock contends: much of its vagueness disappears when it is put into its context. For decades the American courts used the legal expression 'business affected with a public interest' in their judgements and were in complete agreement about what this meant. If they were to do so again, it is likely that the meaning of the expression would be different since the ideological context has changed. But there is no reason to suppose that agreement about what it means would be any less today than it was a hundred years ago. To let politics be guided by one's conception of the public interest is

a spur to conscience and to deliberation. It is a reminder that private rights are not exhaustive of the public interest and that private interests include much more than self-interests. A term that plays this role, even though it lacks precision, is as valuable as it is inescapable. Moreover, in many particular applications, the context of the situation gives the phrase greater definition.[38]

The general assumption of this study is consequently that it is meaningful to try to establish the role of self-interest and public interest in politics, despite the fact that the concepts are very vague and ambiguous. It is not likely that agreement can be reached within the scholarly community on matters of definition or methodology. Here it is presumed, however, that in the great majority of cases it will be possible to make a rough classification of declared motives as either an expression of self-interest or public interest by interpreting them in relation to the context in which they are stated. Our main point concerning the definitions is the following. To think only of the consequences for oneself is an expression of 'self-interest', to think also of others is an expression of 'public interest'—this is probably not a controversial statement. What makes language a bit complicated is that leading public-choice theorists talk about 'short-term self-interest': what actors are supposed to try to achieve is their immediate and personal satisfaction. Against this background, what about a situation when actors find that it is in their own long-term interest to care also for others? In this book such considerations will be classified as a 'public interest'. Decisive for a motive being called 'self-interest' or 'public interest' is consequently if care for others has at all been included in the calculation. Or to put it more technically: the public interest is to promote the common best solution in a 'prisoners' dilemma' by co-operating.

This general point leads in turn to three more detailed premises of the study that might be summed up with the terms rationalism, openness, and empiricism.

Rationalism is the first premiss. It goes without saying that if one attempts to classify the motives of political actors, one has chosen a rationalistic rather than a (natural) scientific mode of explanation. Without assuming that voters and politicians can order their preferences and act in order to realize them, there would of course be no point in analysing the reasons guiding their actions. In contrast to such pioneers of the public-choice school as Downs and Buchanan, however, this study does not equate rational action with selfish action; the term 'rational' is not reserved for those actions which solely serve to satisfy self-interest.[39]

The second premiss of this study is the demand for openness. The point here is simply that the question whether action is to the benefit of only myself or also of others must be left open to test. In accordance with the principle of parsimony, I do not put more into the concepts than is necessary. I defend myself against the charge of egoism, which since the time of Adam Smith has been levelled at those who make use of rational models, by deliberately leaving it open what sort of considerations determine an actor's behaviour. And if it turns out that his motives also include others, it is, of course, rational to act in such a way that this goal can be achieved.[40]

The requirement of such openness contains an element of post-utilitarianism. I have dissociated myself from the view that the public interest automatically emerges from summing up the self-interests of private individuals. The problems of rational choice and of the philosophers listed above should have indicated the doubts that may be had on this score. I also dissociate myself from Dworkin's double-counting thesis, according to which one should only take into consideration personal preferences in politics.[41] When I look into whether self-interest or a conception of the public interest has been of importance for the position a person holds, I shall on the contrary include amongst the possible alternatives 'ethical preferences' or 'convictions'—whatever one wishes to call them. The aim of the study is to investigate whether voters, politicians, and bureaucrats have been influenced not only by their view of what is best for themselves but also by what they believe to be best for others, for the community as a whole.

To answer this question, words and actions will be critically examined. The voting of the elector, the decision-making of the politician, and implementation of the bureaucrat will be compared with their expressed judgements and other assessments. As far as I can see, this enables me to escape being the target of Amartya Sen's ironical comment about behavioural scientists who refrain from communicating with the objects of their interest just as if they were animals without a soul. I try to avoid the mistake of deducing interest from observed behaviour,[42] although I do not find the criticism against doing so to be especially convincing. While it is possible that the older style of aggregate analysis with its sociological and statistical focus could at times have committed this mistake, the situation is radically different for modern political science founded on the survey method: it was, as we have seen, the very possibility of asking questions, of communicating, of interviewing that saved electoral research from the acute methodological difficulties that once confronted it.

This is not to say that all the problems the philosophers raise concerning the determination of a person's view of his own and the general interest have been overcome. Although errors caused by overly superficial observations can hopefully be kept under control, problems remain even with a more intimate approach since the actors may themselves misjudge their own self-interest or even be mistaken about their preferences. To these difficulties there is no general solution. The researcher has no alternative but to assess critically the citizens' statements and the applicability of the data to the question posed in each particular case.

It cannot be denied that a tendency can exist for the requirements of 'rationalism' and 'openness' to conflict with each other. If one is to be completely unprejudiced and prepared to leave all hypotheses open to examination, one should let the assumption of man's rationality also be questioned. All science requires regulative principles, however, and in my analysis of human behaviour, rationalism is the most important of these. Nevertheless, I shall remain as open as possible to a testing of this principle. I shall thus expressly identify situations in which people have acted irrationally. While being faithful to the requirement of closing off as little as possible *a priori* I must nevertheless organize my thoughts according to certain principles, and of these the most important is 'rationalism'.

The third and final premiss of this investigation I call 'empiricism'. This is aimed at an idea that has been given a famous formulation, already cited above, by Anthony Downs in *An Economic Theory of Democracy*: 'Theoretical models should be tested primarily by the accuracy of their predictions rather than by the reality of their assumptions.'[43]

This view, with its roots in American pragmatism, can be interpreted in at least two different ways. The first is as a general statement about which research strategy should be adopted in order to obtain more general knowledge of political reality. As such it is probably no longer controversial within political science. Although in many cases isolated historical studies may still be justified, the main direction of research is to discover less time-bound patterns in political life. For that purpose empirical analyses are surely necessary but they are hardly sufficient. Constructing theories and testing hypotheses are indispensable steps in the research process.

The second interpretation relates to a more sophisticated and questionable idea: that a theory's empirical realism is not as important as its predictive power. Judging by the wording alone it seems most likely to be the second interpretation that Downs had in mind. For the present investigation, one aim of which is to inquire into the empirical basis for the public-choice school's postulate of the predominance of self-interest in politics, such a methodological position would undoubtedly be an embarrassment.

In actual fact, there is no need for alarm. When it comes to engineering or the practical chores of everyday life, a pragmatic criterion of truth may well be warranted: even if a complete causal analysis cannot be carried out, it may still be possible to take measures to achieve the desired effects. One can for example drive a car with no more than a dim notion of how the motor is constructed.

Downs equates explanation with prediction. However, there are many things one can predict without knowing why they occur. One may have found a good indicator but not a good explanation. Basic research is something quite different from such purely instrumental knowledge. One of the aims of basic research is to provide a true description of reality. As a scientist one cannot be satisfied with studying the connection between observed phenomena and predicted outcomes. One must also try to understand the empirical reality that underlies the observations.

The reason why this is necessary has not been explained by anyone with greater authority than Karl Popper. With the interpretation I here put on Downs's statement, his methodology can be identified as the instrumentalism that Popper attacked head on. Galileo's discovery that the movement of the sun across the sky is illusory, a result of the fact that the earth actually moves around the sun, created a new and more accurate conception of the world. Pious men tried as long as they could to present Galileo's theories merely as superior instruments for making calculations. But Galileo persisted in maintaining his view that his theory also presented the world as it truly was, a view that eventually won out until it was succeeded in our own time by the description of reality provided by the theory of relativity.

According to Popper, as is well known, the distinguishing feature of scientific theories is that they can be falsified. Through new observations one can get unexpected results and thereby have reason to revise one's view of reality. What is wrong with instrumentalism is that it can never be falsified. It only sets up rules of thumb of the type 'do such-and-such a thing and this or that will happen'. Instrumentalism can therefore only predict 'events of a kind which is known', while it is a requirement of science to predict 'new kinds of events'. Only science can make new discoveries and thereby give us a truer vision of reality.[44]

The third premiss of this study is thus the Popperian one that there are good reasons to check the empirical basis of a theory. The fact that this view is not completely self-evident, as Downs's statement shows, can possibly account for the Tower of Babel erected within political science in the post-war period: many scholars have held a theory that frees them from the need to worry about the realism of their assumptions. This has given rise to a long list of stimulating hypotheses. But whether these have also given us a truer picture of reality is something we can only know once the theories have been confronted with empirical evidence.

2

Does the Voter Follow His Pocket-Book?

Whether it is self-interest or public interest that is most important to the voter making political choices is something I shall try to determine in this chapter by presenting and discussing a large number of empirical studies. Since American research has predominated in this field both with respect to theory and empirical data, the situation in the USA will be dealt with first. In the following section will be discussed the voters' motives for their choice of party in a number of countries in Western Europe and elsewhere.

As was noted in the introduction, aggregate analysis was the technique most prevalently used in the early period of electoral research during the 1920s and 1930s. This is also true of the particular question that interests us here. Researchers began to ask themselves what importance economic factors have for voting and sought an answer by comparing maps and records of variations in economic and political activity. John Barnhart thus published an analysis of rainfall and votes cast for the Populist Party in the *American Political Science Review* of 1925. Maps showing the size of the population, drought, and the conditions for farming in Nebraska during the 1880s and 1890s were compared with the decline in the number of votes won by the Republican Party and the emergence of the Populist Party. Without succeeding in drawing completely unambiguous results he concluded that the harder times for farming caused by the drought had put the farmers in a 'receptive frame of mind' for the arguments of the populists.[1]

In another pioneering study from the 1920s the correlation between support for the Republican Party and changes in the business cycle was analysed in an electoral district in New Jersey for forty-eight consecutive elections. The author believed he could show that support for the Republican Party increased in good times and declined when the economy slumped.[2]

By this time a model of how such investigations should be carried out had been developed and there followed a large number of studies.[3] For example, one author took the election results from ninety-four districts in the North-Eastern states and set them against fluctuations in economic activity; he maintained that, *ceteris paribus*, the incumbent administration was favoured by economic expansion and was hurt by a depression.

A few other scholars analysed the way in which support for President Roosevelt varied during the 1930s in relation to various economic indicators, especially changes in the trend for wages. A positive correlation was found to exist in three states, a negative one in two. The conclusion they drew was that no systematic relation could be found between economic development and changes in the support for Roosevelt.

In the 1940s Gosnell and Coleman investigated changes in income and voting in the presidential elections in sixty-five counties in Pennsylvania between 1928 and 1936. They found only a weak correlation but this was strengthened with the help of partial correlations.

In a famous book published in the 1940s, *Ballot Behaviour*, Louis Bean compared voting in the congressional elections with changes in the business cycle. The incumbent party lost fifteen of the nineteen elections held during times of recession, with losses in all of the nine elections held without a simultaneous presidential election but only in six of the ten years a presidential election was also held. His conclusion, hardly a sensational one, was that an economic downturn hurts the party in power but that the popularity of the president and other non-economic factors can offset this effect.

Another researcher compared votes for the conservatives over a century (the Whigs, the Republican Party, and the Prohibition Party) with three vaguely defined economic indicators (income per capita, the cost of living, and a price index) and found that there was, at the most, weak support for the hypothesis that economic prosperity leads to conservative votes.

The Swedish researcher, Johan Åkerman, analysed economic depressions and voting in the American presidential elections from 1865 to 1945. He was criticized for arbitrariness in his definitions and classifications when he maintained that sixteen of the twenty elections supported his hypothesis that the president's party loses power in times of depression but keeps it when times are better.

Similar studies were carried out during the 1950s and 1960s as well, but they are much less frequent. One study looked into the connection between the business cycle on the one hand and the share of the vote going to the incumbent president between 1844 and 1948 as well as changes in the parties' strength in Congress between 1856 and 1948 on the other. In neither case could a significant correlation be discovered.

Finally, in an investigation in 1962 the hypothesis concerning the influence of the economy was tested in the congressional elections between 1946 and 1958. The economic variable was measured both in terms of relative unemployment and of farmers' net income. A positive correlation was discovered between voting Republican and low unemployment in slightly more than half of the elections but no correlation between voting and farmers' incomes. The conclusion arrived at was that the Democrats could be said to fare somewhat better in bad times and the Republicans in good.

Through studies of this sort, many scholars contended that they had demonstrated the existence of a phenomenon that was given the name 'economic voting'. Man is primarily a materialistic being who tries to satisfy his economic interests. An earlier, idealized image of the citizen as a person concerned with principle and eager to serve the public interest, an image developed by philosophers without any contact with reality, should now give way to the more realistic view, which had emerged from the empirical studies, that it is primarily self-interest that determines the way a person votes.

Self-interest was thus given a narrowly economic definition. But cannot self-interest show up in other ways? Human beings might concern themselves with power, prestige, sex, appearance etc. That the empirical studies on voting behaviour, political decision-making, and bureaucratic implementation are so oriented towards economics is certainly a problem for any attempt to confront theory and data in the field—the theory being broad and the data too narrow. More comprehensive research on the motives for individual political involvement would be useful. Nevertheless, one can rebut the idea that the concept of self-interest centres on economic matters. This, in turn, suggests that we should take a broader view of the empirical results of research on the matter.

It might be questioned, however, what good reasons there were to adopt the new image of the voter that was now introduced. If one casts a critical eye over the technical-methodological side of the investigations, the strength of the evidence seems far from convincing. Indices and data were put together in a primitive and unsystematic fashion, often without any clear indication of sources or origin. Moreover, as the above account shows, the results were anything but unambiguous. In altogether too many studies the investigators failed to discover the correlation between economics and voting they were looking for, a fact which has caused one author to declare, by way of summing up these studies, that while it certainly appeared as if people voted according to their pocket-book, it was rather embarrassing for political science that there were so many exceptions to this rule.[4]

It is above all the classical ecological fallacy of aggregate analysis that puts these results into doubt. At the level of a geographical unit there is thus shown to exist certain, often not very strong, correlations between economic and political features of the population. What does this tell us about the reasoning of private individuals? That economic factors come into play when a person makes up his mind how he is going to vote seems plausible and is at least not disproved by the studies referred to above. But do these tell us *anything* at all about whether it is self-interest or public interest that has been the decisive motive? Has any given person voted the way he has in order to improve his own lot or out of consideration for the economic development of society as a whole? With their empirical approach, these studies fulfil the third requirement of 'empiricism' that I set up as a premiss for this book (even if the quality in this respect might be questioned in many cases). On the other hand, however, they do not stand up to the requirements of 'rationalism' and 'openness': there is as little attention paid to how individual voters account for their reasons for voting as there is opportunity given them to express their opinion, should they have one, about which political alternative is best for society as a whole. In the words of an author who has surveyed these early studies and discussed their methodological faults: 'And, most importantly, none of these authors make explicit their underlying assumptions about why or how the economy should affect voting. The works are ad hoc empiricism without developed theoretical work presented to support it.'[5]

This problem remained in all essentials when research on economic voting went into its second phase and aggregate analysis made room for survey analysis after the Second World War. There was an improvement in the purely technical quality of the investigations, but the approach of the natural sciences was retained inasmuch as the voters were regarded as being socially and economically determined without any greater capacity for forming independent opinions or acting rationally. In study after study the correlation between income, vocation, education, and other socio-economic variables, on the one hand, and voting, on the other, was confirmed. The theory of class voting was, in short, the latest fashion. The requirement of openness in the testing of hypotheses was not met. No attempt was made to discuss 'altruism' or how the citizen could try to further the public interest, and considering the cynical jargon that began to be widespread, if such an attempt had been made, it would probably have been dismissed with a few sarcastic comments. In the general revision of classical doctrine in survey investigations at that time, it was taken for granted that the voters not only were passive, ignorant, and uninterested in politics but also had a very limited interest in philosophical arguments about what might lie in the public interest.

The major breakthrough for a more modern analysis occurred with the appearance of an article by Gerald Kramer in the *American Political Science Review* in 1971. This work is the point of departure for the very extensive and sophisticated research and debate on economic voting that has since taken place. Interestingly enough, Kramer made use of aggregate data. Even research on economic voting thus kept abreast of the major methodological shifts in electoral research; as was mentioned in Chapter 1 improvements in computers have led to a renewed interest in the possibilities of analysing unwieldy aggregate data. Kramer used data on unemployment and incomes and compared these to voting in congressional elections between 1896 and 1964. He set these into a statistical multivariate model with exemplary care and rigour.

What made this a pioneering effort was above all the fact that Kramer combined this empirical approach with expressly rationalistic assumptions. His actor was 'a rational, self-interested voter' who operated in 'a simple Downsian type of quasi-parliamentary electoral system'. Kramer dismissed the classical view that the citizen without bias collected information on party platforms and the position of the candidates on various questions in order to vote for the one who came closest to sharing his own values. Kramer did not believe that people were willing to devote that much time to politics. He thought it more plausible to assume that the voter bases his considerations on the most easily available information, and that was the performance of the party in power during the latest term of office. It was not altogether easy to interpret the results of this sophisticated analysis. Whereas unemployment was shown to have no effect on election outcomes, an improvement or a deterioration in incomes tended to make the prospects of the party in office better or worse, respectively.[6]

Kramer's article immediately became the object of an extremely critical review by George Stigler, who wished to maintain that the economy had no effect on voting whatsoever, or as he himself described his view: 'our strongly nihilistic conclusions with respect to the influence of general economic conditions on voting behavior'. In short, he confirmed through empirical investigations of his own Kramer's conclusion that unemployment had no effect upon voting but he contended, contrary to Kramer, that changes in wage trends did not have any effect either. In making this analysis he modified Kramer's model in several respects: the minority parties were excluded from the dependent variable; the time period was drawn forward a few years while a few years at the beginning were excluded since data on unemployment in those years were not available; the war years, which Kramer had left out, were included; the statistical calculations were made for two-year intervals instead of four-year intervals; and certain changes were made in the treatment of income statistics.[7] A debate as scholarly as it was heated then ensued.

A couple of years later it was Kramer who found himself in the role of antagonist. He went on the attack against a pair of researchers, Arcelus and Meltzer, who had presented a new empirical analysis of aggregate data on economic voting based on the assumption of rational actors. Their finding was also that economic factors had no direct effects on election outcomes.[8] In collaboration with a colleague Kramer dismissed 'their model, the data they apply it to, the statistical method they use to estimate it, and the way they interpret their results'.[9] A couple of other researchers commented that, in spite of everything, the economy did have an effect on politics but of an asymmetrical nature: the voters punished the party in office for an economic decline but did not reward it for an economic boom.[10] Unconvinced, Arcelus and Meltzer stuck to their view that the theory of economic voting had not received any support from empirical research. 'The work to date has produced mainly null results, our own included.'[11]

Finally, mention should be made in this connection of an article by Edward Tufte, in which he asserted, despite being limited in the number of his observations to a very few cases, that changes in income have an effect on congressional elections.[12] Tufte repeated his claim in a book a few years later. A pair of authors, who were themselves convinced that the economy did not have any effect on presidential elections, wrote of Tufte's work that 'in only one previous analysis have personal finances emerged as a strong predictor of voting decisions'. It was furthermore apparent from Tufte's book that the politicians, at least, believe that the electorate vote on the basis of their pocket-books.[13]

It seems to me, confronted by this rather confusing debate, that the fundamental problem remains unsolved, that it is difficult to answer the question concerning the relative importance of self-interest and public interest with the help of aggregate analysis. This method does not provide any information about the voters' motives for voting as they do. The extensive discussion of technical problems concerning data, variables, models, and statistical methods tends to overshadow the original problem: do the voters look on politics in the light of their principles or do they simply see what personal benefits they can get out of it?

What does an observed correlation between a decline in income *per capita* and a set-back for the incumbent party actually tell us? Is it those who are afflicted who react? Or is the party also abandoned by those who, without having suffered any personal loss, reject the government's economic policy out of consideration for what is best for the society as a whole?[14] That is the vital point in this debate.

If it is the afflicted, we should be entitled to regard the vote as an expression of self-interest. If it is not, the vote should be seen as a sign of public interest. The possibility of interpreting the empirical results in diametrically opposite ways was not foreseen and prevented, a circumstance that brings grist to the philosophers' mill in their claim that, behind all their technical talk, the electoral researchers are not really very bright.

Kramer holds fast to his belief in aggregate analysis. As recently as 1983 he returned to the scene with a defence of the method. One should distinguish between changes in income that depend upon the policy of the government and those that are not so dependent but are rather caused by a person's position in the life cycle or by other non-political conditions, he contends. After all, only the former are relevant to the debate on economic voting. The survey researchers do not observe this distinction. At a higher level of aggregation, on the other hand, changes of the latter sort cancel out each other; for this reason aggregate analysis appears to be the most suitable approach.[15]

By this time, however, the survey researchers had taken over this field of research completely. Survey analysis was considered the only method by which the motives—albeit selfish or altruistic in character—for the citizens' vote could be determined. Or to cite a study published in 1984: 'The basic problem is that the aggregate level studies provide evidence only of covariation between various time series; they cannot examine the mechanisms responsible for the relationships . . . For more direct evidence on this question, researchers turned to survey data to examine the microlevel relationship between economic well-being and political behavior.'[16]

Another researcher pointed out that Kramer's argument for aggregate research should serve rather as an exhortation to the survey researchers to observe the distinction he notes between changes in income caused by different conditions.

What Kramer shows is that if we must choose between individual-level cross-section data with uncorrectable errors and over-time aggregate data with the same weaknesses, the latter are to be preferred in studying economic effects on the vote. But since the aggregate data cannot answer the central question [regarding the respective importance of self-interest and public interest], and probably have biases beyond those Kramer mentions, his result shows only that in the land of the blind, the one-eyed man is king. If depth perception is needed, it may be best to find a new king.[17]

The past decade has been marked by extremely comprehensive survey research on economic voting that satisfies all three of our requirements of rationalism, openness, and empiricism. Practically all of the scholars recognize Kramer's prominence as a pioneer—and ultimately the importance of the assumption of Downs and the rational choice theorists concerning the decisive role of self-interest. But they themselves prefer to work with survey data.

Even a hasty and far from comprehensive run-through of the leading journals and anthologies yields sixty or so titles. Since the debate is continually being fed with new material it might seem hazardous to attempt a general assessment here; an important new work may turn up at any time. However, since the debate is very well integrated with cross-references and marked by an effort towards cumulative knowledge, it is comparatively easy to pick out the most important articles. Fifteen or so of the central studies will be presented below. What indicates that such an effort is worth while is above all the ever-increasing convergence of their results. When it comes to the question of whether the self-interest hypothesis at the centre of attention correctly represents reality or not, survey researchers have moved from an originally rather unclear view to a more and more definite position.

When in 1978 Morris Fiorina began to present his so-called retrospective voting models, in which the voters were asked to look back on changes in their economic situation during the recent past, it was not his results that first attracted attention. His conclusions were mixed. There appeared to be some relation between the voter's private economic situation and his willingness to support the incumbent president. When it came to congressional elections, the correlation was positive only up to 1960 and was negative thereafter. Furthermore, there did not seem to be any correlation between the citizen's economic position and his decision whether or not to participate in the election. Fiorina concluded his article by underlining the preliminary nature of his findings and calling for further research. The fact that he by and large had found little support for his *economic* retrospective voting model did not necessarily mean that the retrospective approach was a mistake; other factors perhaps played a more important role than the economy. 'There are other issues in the world besides the economy, and voters may be reacting to these when they cast their congressional vote . . . To conclude a research report with a call for further study has become a platitude. But given the ambiguity in which this study ends, there is no other way to conclude.'

It was rather his way of tackling the question that aroused interest. Ever since 1956 the pollsters had posed the same question to those they interviewed about their economic situation. Had it improved, deteriorated, or remained the same during the past few years? Fiorina's contribution was to set the answers to these questions systematically in relation to voting behaviour in his model. In this way one should be better able to find an answer to the question of the importance the private individual placed on changes in income when he cast his vote than one could by using the broad generalizations of aggregate analysis.[18]

Other researchers now began to tread the same path. Jeffrey Wides made use of data on private economy and voting intent from electoral surveys in a couple of articles. His results showed that support for the incumbent party increased when there was an improvement in the voter's economic position. Stronger still was the relation between voting and an assessment of the government's economic policy. When control was made simultaneously for the voter's assessment of the policy followed, the parties, and the candidates, the partial correlations between private economy and voting disappeared almost completely. The self-interest hypothesis was confronted with its first rejection from survey research.

The resulting analysis has shown that one's personal economic outlook has little direct influence on the voting decision. It has also shown that the direct impact of evaluations of governmental economic policy is insubstantial. It is the individual and joint effects of evaluations of party and candidate economic competency which directly and substantially influence the vote.[19]

Unemployment is usually considered to be the economic factor of greatest political importance. In 1979 Schlozman and Verba analysed the political consequences of unemployment. During the 1976 presidential elections in the United States, unemployment was higher than it had been at the time of any presidential election since the Depression. It thus provided an excellent opportunity for testing the importance of unemployment for the outcome of the election. It turned out that the unemployed had very little effect on the results. Not only did many of them refrain from voting; those who did divided their votes to a great extent between the candidates. This did not mean that unemployment lacked importance, however. In observing the distinction discussed above, the authors asserted that the attitude of the voters was more important than the actual fact of unemployment. It was not the unemployed but those who held a critical view of the level of unemployment who turned away from the governing party.

Thus, our findings are consistent with the hypothesis that unemployment has potential for influencing national electoral outcomes, but that the effect comes, not from the unemployed themselves, but from others who vote in accordance with their opinions on unemployment as an issue . . . Political activity is more a function of beliefs about politics than of specific personal experiences; political beliefs, in turn, are more a function of general social beliefs than of personal experiences.[20]

The scientists now began to refine their analyses by studying subgroups. A deeper insight into the implications of economic voting than that springing from the debate between aggregate researchers and survey researchers could be achieved, Stephen Weatherford maintained, if one were to study the behaviour of social groups. While there perhaps did not exist much support for the self-interest hypothesis within the middle class, the working class, which was harder hit by a decline in the economy, also reacted more strongly in the elections.[21] Opposition candidates were little affected by the state of the economy but the candidates for the incumbent party were more sensitive to a downturn in the business cycle, Hibbing and Alford showed.[22]

The view was becoming accepted that survey analysis was superior to aggregate analysis because its unit of analysis was smaller. But could not the same advantages be achieved by breaking down the national aggregates? The 'business cycle' was after all far from being a uniform phenomenon: in certain areas there might be a recession while in others the economy could be booming. Owens and Olson therefore carried out an analysis at the electoral-district level using aggregate data. They studied 429 elections spread over three election years. It might be objected against this 'disaggregated' analysis that while it certainly registers regional variations in the independent variable with sensitivity, it retains the fundamental inability to distinguish between 'afflicted' and 'merely convinced'.

At all events, the result was not in favour of the self-interest hypothesis. 'Economic concerns do not translate into voting behavior . . . The voting decision is not simply a choice based upon economic preferences.'[23]

A philosopher cast himself into the fray. Unfolding his argument in the form of a dialogue, Paul Meehl maintained that if one were to believe the view held by Downs, Buchanan, and other public-choice theorists concerning the voters' egoism, the fact that the voters participated at all appeared completely inexplicable and irrational. There was no reason to vote, for the individual could not exert any appreciable impact on the outcome. The influence or exchange gained was not proportional to the effort made. Refuting his imaginary opponent, Meehl argued that a vote for a small third party was no more of a 'thrown-away' vote than one for one of the large parties. For, as he had already shown, a vote for one of the big two did not give the individual much influence either; the candidate would in all likelihood win or lose quite independently of this single vote. The problem with the assumption of self-interest as a motive for voting, as with much of the theorizing of the public-choice school, was in Meehl's view the inaptness of the parallel between political and economic activity. A rational person buys a hamburger because he is hungry, not because he wants to influence the macro-process of supply, demand, and price. But a vote is not in the same way a guarantee that one gets what one wants, i.e. that the particular candidate one chooses gets elected. In voting, all one does is participate in a macro-process, hardly a rewarding occupation. Egoism cannot explain why people bother to vote. Altruism offers a better answer. People vote because they are concerned about other people. Meehl suggested the term 'sociotropic' to denote this attitude. A desire to further the public interest was seen as a better explanation of voting than the self-interest hypothesis.[24] The new term became quickly established in the debate.

Kinder and Kiewiet asserted in a long article that 'with respect to economic issues, voters appear to choose between congressional candidates "sociotropically". Voters are not egocentric in any narrow sense: they do not vote their *own* pocketbooks. Rather, their preferences follow a more collective reckoning.' Behind these conclusions lay survey data from the elections of 1956–76. However, the researchers did not simply analyse the usual questions about changes in the private economic situation and party preferences of the persons interviewed, but also included more general matters such as their opinion of the state of the country's economy, of the parties' competence when it came to fighting inflation and unemployment, and of the economic policy followed by the government. In this respect it must be said that our second requirement of theoretical openness was more than adequately met: the citizens had not only been given an opportunity to express their self-interest but also a chance to declare some conviction about what was best for the country as a whole. The relation between all these factors was calculated in a statistical model with the result that the self-interest hypothesis was rejected.

In short, our evidence argues forcefully against the personal grievances explanation for the relationship between economic conditions and congressional election outcomes . . . The link appears to be provided, instead, by voters reaching decisions based partly on their collectively-oriented economic judgments . . . These collective economic judgments seem surprisingly independent of privately experienced economic discontents.'[25]

In 1981 the same authors continued this line of argument in the celebrated article 'Sociotropic Politics: The American Case'. They began by studying a number of congressional elections in the United States of the 1970s. Throughout, they compared the 'pocket-book hypothesis' with the 'sociotropic hypothesis'. But how sharply is a voter's view of his private economic situation separated from his assessment of the state of the country's economy? This aspect of the problem was not neglected by the authors. 'The reader may wonder at this point about the relationship between pocketbook discontents and sociotropic judgments. Are assessments of national economic conditions anything more than generalization of the economic trials and tribulations of private life? They certainly are. Connections between the two are in fact surprisingly tenuous.' When these were then related to voting behaviour, it turned out that a person's private economic experience had very little impact on his choice of candidate in the congressional elections whereas his sociotropic judgements were of the utmost importance.

Following this, a similar analysis of the presidential election of 1976 was carried out. The same pattern emerged: the pocket-book hypothesis was actually given even less support than in the congressional elections. The conclusion was expressed in no uncertain terms: 'According to the evidence presented here, American voters resemble the sociotropic ideal, responding to changes in general economic conditions, much more closely than the pocketbook ideal, responding to the circumstances of personal economic life.'

In concluding their study the authors reflected on the implications of this insight. A socio-psychological explanation could be found in terms of American individualism. The American citizen did not blame others or society for his personal economic difficulties. He put the blame on his own shoulders. For the state of the country's economy, however, he held the President and politicians responsible.[26]

In *Macroeconomics and Micropolitics* (1983) Kiewiet provides the fullest statement of his position. He repeats his scepticism about the self-interest hypothesis and emphasizes the fact that Americans tend to attribute their own economic fortunes to forces other than the government. Both personal experiences and national assessments are taken into account when voters make up their minds. 'Of the two, however, it is national assessments which have the greater electoral consequences.'[27]

Working with different collaborators, David Sears published a few articles in which he tested the self-interest hypothesis, which for once was not defined in strictly economic terms. Nor did he assess the merits of the hypothesis against those of what we normally think of first when we hear the term 'public interest'. Sears compared self-interest with what he called 'symbolic politics', i.e. a process through which one's political attitude is brought into harmony with one's fundamental values, which are established early in life and have nothing whatsoever to do with how much one stands to gain or lose personally on some issue. In one study, the attitudes amongst whites to the busing of schoolchildren was analysed. It was shown that the opinion held by people on this issue was independent of whether they themselves had children who were bused, while symbolic attitudes in terms of racism and political conservatism were decisive. Relating these findings to the literature, the authors polemized against the self-interest hypothesis that had emerged after Downs.[28]

In a further study, symbolic politics was set against self-interest in four issue areas (unemployment, health insurance, busing, and crime). Once again the self-interest hypothesis was rejected. 'In general, symbolic attitudes . . . had strong effects, while self-interest had almost none.'[29]

In more recent years the descriptive question of what sort of motive mainly guides the American voter has been supplemented to an ever greater extent with methodological analyses and a discussion of the causes and emergence of these motives. Sears and Lau showed in a special study that much of the empirical support that had been referred to in support of the self-interest hypothesis was an artefact: political preferences had been privatized by the researchers by being related to the household economy of the person interviewed; assessments of his private economic situation had been politicized by being made directly after expressed political preferences. In reality, however, such a relation between the private and the public seldom existed. 'This link is normally not salient enough to give American political preferences much of a self-interested base.'[30]

One scholar deprecated the tendency to set hypotheses against each other as mutually exclusive alternatives; the private individual was probably affected by both types of consideration, although to different degrees. The author suggested therefore that the hypotheses be regarded as the poles of a continuum on which the mixture of motives of a particular individual might be placed. As sane and sensible as this suggestion may seem, however, it gives us very little help in finding the answer to the question of whether it is self-interest or public interest that is more significant in determining the voter's choice.[31]

Had the time come to write off the self-interest hypothesis completely as an explanation to voting behaviour? No, answered Sigelman and Yung-Mei Tsai. One could think of at least four shortcomings that prevented the self-interest hypothesis from emerging in the research that had been carried out up to then: it was not reasonable to hold the rulers responsible for the economy except in presidential elections; all aspects of private economic life had not been examined; the much-debated theory of asymmetry, according to which afflicted voters punished the politicians while favoured voters did not necessarily reward them, should receive more consideration and might afford the self-interest hypothesis a better chance; and self-interest should not be limited to economic advantages. The authors then carried out extensive empirical studies in which these factors were taken into consideration. Nevertheless their findings failed to support the self-interest hypothesis. 'In sum, even when all the plausible theoretical and methodological factors that could have undermined the ability of personal finances to predict voting decisions are considered and corrected, the linkage between personal finances and voting choices remains minimal at best.'[32]

Another study started from Kramer's defence of aggregate analysis but asserted, as a researcher mentioned above immediately did in reply to Kramer, that even survey research should consider the fact that some of the factors affecting the personal economic situation of an individual obviously occur through no fault of the government and should therefore, have no effect on the outcome of the elections. When it was controlled with the help of advanced statistical methods, the sociotropic image of the American voter was quite appreciably weakened.[33]

On the other hand, yet another study showed that even if it can be demonstrated that the pocket-book hypothesis fits pretty well in certain cases—not for all voters but for those who have become worse off—the sociotropic hypothesis provides a better explanation of the election result even in these cases, quite simply because the number of voters who have become worse off does not vary very much from one election to the next.[34]

In most studies a picture thus emerges of the voter as someone primarily guided by a concern for the economy of the country as a whole. What gives rise to this sociotropic behaviour? That is the question Stanley Feldman has discussed in a couple of articles that contain both a critique of the literature and a presentation of his own findings. Like Kinder and Kiewiet, Feldman looks for the answer in the economic liberalism of the United States; Americans do not blame the politicians for their financial failures. Private economic experience does not make much of an impact on public affairs. 'The accumulated evidence very strongly suggests that vote choice and presidential evaluations are at best modestly influenced by *personal* economic considerations . . . Personal self-interest is typically not a major element in studies of political behavior.'[35]

Abramowitz reports that neither what the voter believed about his personal economic situation nor what he believed about the national economy turned out to have any *direct* effect upon his vote; his assessment of the President's record was more important. Through multiple analysis an indirect effect appeared, however: economic judgements influenced an assessment of the President, more particularly and quite logically, judgements pertaining to the economy of the country as a whole. 'Expectations regarding the future of the national economy had by far the strongest impact on Reagan evaluations.'[36]

And finally, in a piece in 1986, Feldman together with a few other authors wonders what role party identification has to play in the forming of sociotropic motivation, for some scholars consider that a person's attitude towards the economy is only a reflection of party bias: government supporters might be expected to have a rather rosy view of the national economy, the opposition's supporters a dismal one. However, as Abramowitz's article also shows, it is the state of the economy that influences political evaluations of the President rather than partisanship that gives the voter a biased view of the national economy. The voters' assessment of inflation and unemployment turned out in fact to be quite accurate. 'Specifically, we find no evidence that retrospective assessments of inflation and unemployment are significantly affected by partisan dispositions.'[37]

To sum up, it is remarkable how difficult and complicated it has been to find an answer to the question whether the American voter is primarily guided by self-interest or public interest when he casts his vote. We started from the straightforward premiss that this question, the object of such prolixity, could be answered by looking into the results of electoral studies. Instead we became bogged down by a debate on method in which the most divergent opinions contended with each other and in which the slightest variation in data or definitions could lead to dramatically different results. However, when research into economic voting eventually followed a path that provided an adequate treatment of the hypotheses of self-interest and public interest, a clearer picture gradually emerged. Despite a few remaining moot points, the results point overwhelmingly against the self-interest hypothesis. The electoral behaviour of American voters can best be characterized as 'sociotropic'. They do not vote in the first place according to their pocket-books but rather for the alternative they believe to be best for the country as a whole.

WESTERN EUROPE AND OTHER STATES

In recent Western European electoral research the same picture has begun to merge as in the United States: electors who in their voting are more affected by the way the government manages the national economy than by their personal financial situation.[38] This research is highly influenced by the American example. Just about everywhere where a parliamentary election takes place there are political scientists on the spot with their questionnaires to trace the causes of shifts in the attitudes of the voters. In many countries the question of economic voting has been raised in this connection. Unfortunately most of these studies do not go any further than the general relation between economics and politics (is it unemployment, inflation, or the budget deficit that carries the most weight and what consequences do various levels in these variables have for the ballot box?), often citing Harold Wilson's comment that a government's chances of winning an election depend on how successful its economic policy has been.[39] However, despite what others sometimes imply, to establish this general relation is not the same thing as to produce evidence for the self-interest hypothesis. To do that, one must work instead with an open model able to distinguish 'pocket-book' motives from 'sociotropic' motives and one must succeed in showing that the former are more important than the latter.

The few European researchers who do work in this acceptable way have a tendency to repeat the mistakes of the Americans. The Europeans have had noticeable difficulty in refraining from calculating simple correlations when the American researchers have already demonstrated how necessary it is to penetrate the material more deeply to be sure that the observed pattern reflects actual conditions. To avoid tiresome repetition, I shall not recapitulate the methodological criticism already put forward in connection with the American studies, but rather concentrate on a presentation of the results.

Against this background it should hardly surprise the reader that the most important work on the economic voting of Western European voters has been written by an American. In 1986 Michael Lewis-Beck at the University of Iowa published an article on 'Comparative Economic Voting: Britain, France, Germany, Italy' in the *American Journal of Political Science*. On account of the care taken by the author, the methodological sophistication of his presentation, and the scope of his empirical results, this article deserves a more extensive reference.

The author began by noting the great predominance of aggregate analyses in studies of European economic voting. The Europeans had not followed the lead of the Americans and turned to survey data to overcome their methodological difficulties, however. Thanks to Europa-Barometer, a public opinion institute that has conducted regular studies since 1973, there existed at the individual level both election data and a large amount of other information for Great Britain, France, West Germany, and Italy that had been collected in October 1983.

In connection with the great American debate the author set out the four dimensions of the voter's view of the relation between economics and politics. The first corresponded with the principal question of the present study: self-interest or public interest. The second pertained to whether judgements were direct or indirect ('simple or mediated'). The former consisted in the voter's opinion of whether unemployment, inflation, etc., were higher, lower, or unchanged in comparison with the previous year. The latter related to the voter's view of the government's responsibility: did the voter consider that it was the policy pursued by the government that caused unemployment, inflation, etc. to be higher, lower, or unchanged in comparison with the previous year. The third dimension concerned retrospective judgements, in which the voter reflected on the past, or prospective judgements, in which he looked into the future. The fourth dimension, finally, took up cognitive as opposed to affective judgements: 'prices are going up' in contrast with 'the way the government looks after the economy makes me angry'.

These four dimensions were combined in different ways in eleven questions and the correlations between the answers to these and voting behaviour were calculated for all four countries. The general picture that resulted confirmed the fact that the state of the economy in a country does have an effect on the election results. Significantly, no correlation could be found between variables of the greatest importance to our study: the relation between the voter's personal economic situation and his vote.

The findings support the general notion that the citizens of Britain, France, Germany, and Italy are economic voters. Deteriorating economic situations appear to push these voters to the opposition. The coefficients of the economic variables are generally in the expected direction and statistically significant, with the important exception of those from the household financial situation variable. Surprisingly, in none of the countries does this personal variable produce a coefficient significant at the .05 level. An implication is that selfish pocketbook considerations do not directly enter into the calculations of the Western European voter.

Nevertheless, the author did not wish to discard the self-interest hypothesis so lightly. Was it not possible that personal finances could have an *indirect* effect on voting? If the voters hold the government responsible for the economic development of the country, would it not be reasonable for them to punish or reward the incumbent party? Raising this question one runs up against a further complication. If it is parties that are to be put in the balance, then one must also take into consideration other political factors that bear upon partisan attitudes, factors such as class membership and party identification. Lewis-Beck therefore incorporated both of these factors into his analysis of economic voting. The result was devastating for the self-interest hypothesis all the same:

we believed that, even though a *simple* evaluation of personal finances could not influence the vote, *mediated* evaluation could, because it explicitly allowed the attachment of government responsibility to personal economic circumstances. Nevertheless, the more properly specified model . . . shows such is not the case . . . Our conclusion about the presence of pocketbook voting in Western European electorates can now be stated more broadly, and more confidently: personal retrospective economic considerations, either simple or mediated, do not exercise a direct effect on the vote.

Not content with this result, the author was untiring in seeking further possibilities that might lend support to the self-interest hypothesis. Perhaps the influence of personal economic circumstances was even more subtle than had generally been supposed. Lewis-Beck turned to re-examine his retrospective and prospective questions.

At this stage he was thus trying to keep many balls up in the air at the same time. However, from studies of economic voting in the United States, political scientists have learnt to manage such multivariate analyses. It is possible for example to determine not only what influences voting behaviour but also what influences those factors which influence voting. Anyone can see, however, that even in such a complex set of issues as this, some variables must be endogenous with respect to others. After extensive calculations Lewis-Beck expressed his final conclusion as follows.

Of all the economic variables, the only one that does not perform as expected is the personal SRE [Simple Retrospective Evaluations], which asks about the financial situation of the household. In none of these countries does the perception of a worsening financial situation at home significantly increase the likelihood of a negative evaluation of government economic management. Nor . . . does it so relate to future expectations about such government actions. The absence of these indirect effects reinforces our earlier conclusion that the voter's perception of his or her past financial circumstance, in and of itself, has no impact on the vote.

By way of conclusion the author pondered over some of the differences between the four countries studied. Economic voting, in the sense of consideration for the economic welfare of the country as a whole, had the greatest impact on voting in Great Britain, followed by West Germany and France, and had the least impact in Italy. One reason for this was perhaps the fact that the British government had a reputation of looking after the economy efficiently and responsibly, something which the author apparently considered must be true to a diminishing extent for West Germany, France, and Italy, respectively. He speculated further over the difference between a two-party system like the British, in which it was easier to perceive an opposition, and a multi-party system, in which responsibility and protest-voting are more diffuse phenomena. Finally, the author suggested that it was conceivable that more traditional factors, such as class, religion, and membership of a political party, play a larger role in countries like Italy and France than in Great Britain.[40]

This awareness of the weakness of the self-interest hypothesis in explaining European voting has only been reached after a long and tortuous route. Great Britain has the longest tradition of survey research, almost as long as the United States, with David Butler as its leading figure. Butler began as early as 1951 and has subsequently carried out a great number of studies of British elections in conjunction with various co-authors. *Political Change in Britain* (1969), a book he wrote with Donald Stokes, an American from the Michigan group, which despite some controversy has established itself as the best electoral study to come out of Great Britain, attracts special interest in the present context because of its analysis of the impact of economic variables on politics. According to the authors of this book, economic policy constitutes a special case for the voters since they do not pass judgement on issues of principle so much as assess the purely technical competence of the political parties to bring about economic growth, which all wish to further. The fact that the voters consequently punish a government for poor times and reward them for good also emerges clearly from this study.

Butler and Stokes did not overlook the distinction between economic self-interest and an interest in the economic state of the country as a whole. It is the latter, they maintained, that stands at the focus of the public debate, and they declared that they would therefore be very surprised if it should turn out that the health of the country's economy only influenced the vote of those whose personal financial situation had been affected. Sure enough, the voters were revealed to look further than to their own finances. The authors compared three curves. Two of them referred to the voter's personal economic situation and were remarkably flat: one described assessments of whether the voter's economic situation had improved or deteriorated, the other perceptions of whether the government had contributed to this economic improvement or deterioration. By contrast, the third curve, which was designed to capture opinions of the way the government had managed the economic problems of the country as a whole, swung dramatically over time. In other words, changes in the government's reputation of being able to manage the country's finances could not be explained by the way people experienced changes in the economy of their household. The individual voter's perception of the general competence of the government in the field of economic policy went further in accounting for the way he voted than did any change in his personal finances.

In view of the very real effects which changes in the economy have on the lives of ordinary people, many observers have naturally assumed that economic change is translated into party support by the shifts of those whose economic lot has been worsened or improved. On this view, the political impact of changes in the economy is simply aggregated out of the individual decisions of those whose well-being has been affected. But there are reasons to be sceptical about such a view. For one thing, the shifts of party support that have been associated with economic changes have been larger than could be explained by summing together such individual effects. The ebbs and flows of the party tide have, for example, been far greater than the numbers of people who have entered or left the ranks of the unemployed.

The economic time-series that best coincided with voters' party preferences was actually that for the balance of payments, something which also lent support to the view that the voters give greater weight to the state of the economy of the nation as a whole than to their personal financial situation when casting their vote.

Clearly, those who perceive governments as affecting their individual economic position do tend to vote accordingly. But there was remarkably little variation over the decade in the fraction of the electorate which formed such perceptions. The great majority of the electorate did not feel that its lot had been worsened by the Conservatives in 1963. Neither did it feel that its lot had been improved by Labour in 1966 or worsened by Labour in 1968 and 1969. To be sure, there was some variation of this sort, but it could not account for more than a part of the impact of economic change. The economy is, however, a collective or national issue as well as an individual issue, and governments gain or lose support according to their perceived success in dealing with the economy as a whole.[41]

The argument of Butler and Stokes can be said to give general support to the public-interest hypothesis rather than the self-interest hypothesis but their test is far more tentative and indirect than that employed by Lewis-Beck in his pithy analyses. The same might be said of most British studies of economic voting, which have grown over the years to a considerable number owing to the exceptional preoccupation of the British with the economic problems that have plagued them since the Second World War: the dissolution of the Empire, chronic crisis, and decline. In *The Politics of Economic Decline* for example, which was also written by an American, James Alt writes by way of introduction of how, during the decade he lived in Great Britain, he was struck by the similarity between the economy and the weather: neither of them were as good as people wished, everyone was constantly talking about them, and nobody ever did anything about them. Time and time again, however, when he took up the question of 'altruism' and 'egoism' in politics to give an account of how the British regard their personal economic situation, the financial state of the nation, and the ability of the political parties to govern the country, the author contented himself with a comparatively simple measure. In the choice between less unemployment for the benefit of the minority of unemployed and lower inflation for the benefit of all (albeit to varying degrees), the former was designated as the altruistic choice and also turned out to be the one favoured by the British voters. The rationale behind using this as a measure of altruism was that the number of people who favoured a reduction in unemployment was considerably greater than the number of those who were worried lest they themselves became unemployed.[42]

When it comes to West Germany certain questions of economic policy can be plucked from the well-documented German electoral studies. The most penetrating analysis has recently been presented in a large survey article on the self-interest and public interest of the German voter. The analysis is based on data from no less than twenty-five survey studies from the period 1961 to 1984. The author pays special attention to the relation between the economic judgements of the voters and their party preferences since it seemed likely that part of the co-variation between voting behaviour and these judgements could be traced to a common background factor: party preference. Control for this factor was thus made and the author gives a detailed description of what the correlation looks like. Even when the influence of party preference is taken into account in this fashion, however, it turns out that the voter's assessment of the economic situation of the country as a whole is more significant than the state of his personal finances for the way he casts his vote. In summing up his findings, the author writes: 'collective economic judgments are generally a more potent predictor of electoral choice than individual economic judgments'.[43]

When it comes to the French elections it is not as easy to find relevant survey studies; the ecological tradition with observations aggregated by geographical units lives on in this country. As a matter of fact, it is Lewis-Beck who has written the most significant articles, even though they do not delve as deep as the comparative analysis cited above. In these earlier works on economic voting in France Lewis-Beck wrote of influence both from the voter's personal situation and the voter's view of the economy of the country at large, something which was considered a contrast to the American studies which almost without exception, it was claimed, supported the public interest hypothesis. Why did such a difference exist between these two countries? Lewis-Beck referred to the cultural explanation already discussed above:[44] Americans profess themselves proponents of economic liberalism and blame themselves for their set-backs whereas the French (who according to Lewis-Beck are less individualistic) hold the government responsible to a greater extent for some misfortune in their private affairs.

Such a tentative explanation is quite evidently little more than speculation of about the same sort as Lewis-Beck's none too convincing reflections in his comparative study of the causes of variations in the economic voting of four countries. As the author himself was later to demonstrate, this attempt to salvage the self-interest hypothesis was unnecessary, for it is as little supported by the data for French voters as for American.[45]

Research on the rest of Europe is rather patchy. The young Spanish democracy has been studied along all four of Lewis-Beck's dimensions. The results show consistently that the effect of personal financial circumstances, both 'simple' and 'mediated', are of considerably less significance than assessments of the way the government has managed the economy of the country as a whole. The authors could thus draw the conclusion that the pattern found elsewhere is repeated in Spain:

Once voters take the multiple aspects of economic policy and performance into account, their own personal financial situation bears little on their vote choice . . . Interestingly, this finding squares with survey work from the United States and other Western European countries which reports that, contrary to expectations, simple 'pocket-book' voting is weak to nonexistent.[46]

In Austria the same pattern is found. The voters' view of the general economic situation in the country is far more important for the way they vote than their personal financial circumstances, which have almost no significance at all on the choice of party.[47]

Concerning the Dutch voter it has only been possible to find a very specialized study in which changes in political thinking and vote are classified. While the first way of thinking is said to proceed from 'personal experience' and the second from the interests of the 'group' with which one identifies, the third is ideological and refers to 'collective values'. Empirical data on voters show a widening of perspective from the 1960s, when it was clearly group-oriented, towards a more ideological form of thinking in the 1970s and 1980s.[48]

In Sweden systematic electoral studies have been carried out by the Department of Political Science at the University of Gothenburg since the end of the 1950s. This research constitutes the most extensive and detailed series of studies outside the United States. The results of the Swedish data support the public-interest hypothesis. For example, in one of the most recent reports Sören Holmberg developed a detailed argument on economic voting. He first asked if those who have met with difficulties because of the deterioration in the job market tend to abandon the government in the elections. It turned out they do, but the correlation was comparatively weak. If the voters' occupational group (a strong determinant of party preference) was taken into consideration, a large part of the correlation disappeared.

The next part of the analysis dealt with the well-known question of the effect on voting of the voter's assessment of whether he has become financially better or worse off over the past few years. The correlation emerged more clearly here. Holmberg was suspicious of these results, however. In contrast to another study mentioned above, the material indicated that the partisan loyalties of the voters truly did bias the picture they gave of changes in their personal economic situation; thus, for example, strongly convinced Social Democrats maintained to a greater extent than Social Democrats with weaker affinity for the party that they had become worse off under the non-socialist governments. An analysis of party-switching strengthened Holmberg's suspicions regarding the voters' self-judgements; the voter's assessment of his own economic development did not give rise to any markedly greater likelihood of switching party bloc. The conclusion he came to was that the fact of being worse off economically did affect voting but the effect was not particularly strong.

The most interesting thing about our results is perhaps not the discovery that there exists at the voter level certain correlations between economic change and voting. What is interesting is rather that the correlations are so weak. Changes in the voters' financial situation were not an especially important factor in accounting for their vote in 1982. Economic self-interest was an explanatory factor but it was not a significant explanatory factor.

Holmberg also examined how the voters' apportioned blame to the various governments for the crisis in the national economy, to see if this related to changes in their own personal finances and voting behaviour. Once again the self-interest hypothesis received no more than weak support. 'The independent effect on voting of changes in the voters' personal financial situation was very limited beside the effect of the voters' assessment of the parties' economic policy.'

Holmberg sums up the relation between economics and politics as follows. His analyses have shown

very clearly that the interrelation [between economics and politics] in 1982 was primarily dependent upon the fact that the economy was one of the central issues in the election and that the voters' assessments of the economic policies of the various parties influenced voting. The interplay between the economy and party choice depended to a very slight extent on the fact that the voters looked to the way their own finances had changed, punishing the government party if they had become worse off and rewarding it if they had become better off. Our results thus show that there is obviously a connection between economics and politics at the voter level as well. But the main link connecting economic change to voting behaviour is not primarily the voters' short-term economic self-interest but rather their broader assessments of the country's economy and of the financial policies of the various parties.[49]

In an earlier report Holmberg made the question of the self-interest or public interest of the voters a special object of study. In the Swedish election of 1979, the closing days of the campaign focused to a large extent on the taxation of private houses. Holmberg could show that the vote of the house-owners was not at all as uniform as many had thought. On the contrary, there were individual house-owners who were sympathetic to the proposal to limit the right of house-owners to claim tax deductions for their mortgage costs, just as there were conservative tenants who considered that house-owners should be allowed to keep their right to deductions. The ideological factor was somewhat more important in determining attitudes than the fact of whether one owned a house or not. The voter's self-interest was less important than his ideological position.[50]

Again in his latest report on the Swedish election of 1985 Holmberg and his associates reject the self-interest hypothesis of voter behaviour. It was the voters' assessment of how the economy of the country had developed, not of how their personal financial situation had changed, that was most strongly connected to the way they voted.

To the extent that the voters' private finances played any role at all in determining the vote in 1985, their effect was weak and went indirectly via the voters' assessments of economic policies in the light of the state of the country's economy. This result is hardly surprising. Sören Holmberg made a very similar finding when he studied the relation between the voters' economic assessments and their vote in the election of 1982. In neither 1982 nor 1985 was the state of the voter's personal finances an important factor behind his choice of party. Of course, there were voters who looked into their pocket-books before they voted. But most did not do so. Instead they followed their assessments in terms of economic policy of how the Swedish economy had developed. And this they did regardless of whether they themselves had become worse off or better off financially over the past few years.[51]

Axel Hadenius has looked into the attitude of the Swedes towards their taxes. Three models were tested: the self-interest hypothesis, the public-interest hypothesis (in the form of 'political attitudes', such as position on the ideological continuum from left to right and general opinion of politicians and authorities), and the notion of 'political resources' (education, organizational affiliation, ability to appeal against the decisions of authorities, etc.). Political attitudes turned out to be completely decisive for discontentment with taxes; for the self-interest hypothesis and the whole theoretical framework from which it is derived the results were disappointing. 'Public-choice supporters thus feeling disappointed may possibly find consolation in the fact that the political resources have an even poorer result', writes the author good-naturedly in rounding off his study.[52]

Concerning the Norwegian voter there are a number of interesting studies available. In an analysis of the motives for tax evasion, the self-interest hypothesis, according to which well-informed and utility-maximizing citizens are presumed to react to objective elements of the taxation system, was tested against the public-interest hypothesis. In this case the hypothesis was formed in line with the notion of 'symbolic politics', i.e. basic attitudes independent of one's personal advantage. An aggregate-level analysis of the United States and eleven Western European countries was first carried out. The self-interest hypothesis was given a specific interpretation: tax evasion should be more tolerated in countries with high levels of taxation than in others. This hypothesis received little support; in Sweden, for example, the country with the highest level of taxation, attitudes towards tax evasion were also the most restrictive, while in Spain, with a low level of taxation, they were generally tolerant. In the second stage of the study, Norwegian survey data were introduced, whereupon it turned out that symbolic politics explained attitudes towards tax evasion far better than the self-interest hypothesis. This result was further supported by the fact that political interest tended to reinforce tax morality.[53]

These scholars have also conducted a special study of Lewis-Beck's theory, mentioned above, of the cultural differences between the United States and Western Europe. But they have not been able to find anything in their Norwegian data to support the notion that the voters' personal finances have a greater impact on voting than it does amongst American voters.[54]

Finally, the same research group put forward an excellent example of the main approach to the study of economic voting. The parliamentary elections during 1965–85 were made the object of a penetrating analysis in which the greater number of the many subtle methodological points mentioned above were observed. Once again the self-interest hypothesis was rejected.

Overall, the results for the individual economic items suggest that pocket book voting is not widespread in Norwegian elections . . . The results for the personal items are especially disappointing for those that see the outcome of an election as determined by calculations of personal economic costs and benefits, and election day as a time for punishing or rewarding the responsible parties for one's good or bad fortunes . . . Personal economic concerns do not seem to be of great importance at Norwegian elections.[55]

Danish research in this area, unlike the Norwegian, does not lie in the mainstream of the debate. Nevertheless, it gives general support to the image of a voter who is motivated rather by socio-political than selfish economic concerns. Like the Dutch study referred to above, Danish research has declared there to be an increase in the share of 'ideologically' guided voters at the expense of what are termed 'utilitarian'.[56]

To conclude, let us look at a couple of other democracies outside the United States and Western Europe. The picture in Canada appears at first glance to be contradictory. Besides a couple of traditional studies that reject the self-interest hypothesis in the usual fashion—about which more below—there is also one article that comes to the directly opposite conclusion. Of all the sources on which this chapter is based, it is in fact the one study that most clearly comes down in favour of the self-interest hypothesis: the findings are said to be 'more consistent with a personal experience than with a sociotropic interpretation'. However, a closer examination of the article reveals that the author avails himself of a somewhat peculiar terminology. By 'self-interest' he thus means 'enlightened self-interest', which can also entail improvements for one's fellows. It is expressly stated that 'a distinction will not be made between altruism and enlightened self-interest'. The definition appears to be an artefact of the way in which J. R. Happy has set up his study (aggregate analysis with observations by region for the fifteen federal elections between 1930 and 1979) and cannot, as the author himself concedes, yield any separate direct measurements with regard to personal economic or sociotropic motives. In this respect the study does not fulfil our requirement of 'openness' in the construction of the model and can only provide information about whether the Canadian voters acted wisely in the light of their own and others' best interests in economic terms. The conclusion thus has a different connotation from that implied by the terms themselves.[57]

In another article is presented a survey study of support for the Canadian government in 1954 and 1979. After analysing the data the author came to the conclusion that the ideas of Anthony Downs and his followers must be rejected. The voters did not see any decisive difference between the economic policies of the various parties and their support for the parties was comparatively unaffected by economic conditions. The choice of party sprang from other, more political, motives than changes in the economic circumstances of the voters. 'These findings thus do not confirm the Downsian referendum scenario suggesting that political support is a simple response to economic conditions, with good times rallying the public behind the incumbent party and bad times causing the public to indicate their desire for a change in economic conditions by supporting the Opposition.'[58]

The question of self-interest *versus* sociotropy is also dealt with in a larger work on public opinion and politics recently published in Canada. There it is argued that the voters' personal finances are not insignificant for their views on the country's economy but the explanatory power of this factor is weak. The main impression the book leaves one with is that the voters' assessments of the general economic state of the country are largely independent of their personal experiences. The voters also vote, strangely enough, directly against their self-interest: the government has received greater support the worse the state of the economy has been![59]

Despite cultural differences Japanese voters have also come to be described with the help of models of economic voting. The result for the self-interest hypothesis has been as equally devastating here as in the United States or Western Europe. In an analysis of the correlation between certain conditions and support for the governmental party in one of the world's best run economies, the coefficients were not only weak but also in the opposite direction to what one would have reason to expect on the basis of the theory. Inflation and unemployment did not hurt the government, nor did increases in income favour it. 'This finding firmly supports the predictions of the global judgment model and discredits the personal grievance model. The evidence indicates that individuals do not vote their own money problems but instead respond to how the government is handling the economy in general.'[60]

The comparative research on economic voting can be summed up in the words of a leading authority who, in a work on the state of knowledge about a large number of countries, notes that there is general agreement on the fact that sociotropic assessments are significant for voting behaviour yet the pocket-book hypothesis is still debated. What keeps the discussion alive is not the discovery of any evidence to support it but rather the fact that it seems so plausible: 'a good hypothesis facing resistant data'.[61]

CONCLUSIONS

How would sceptical philosophers regard these results of electoral research? Would they agree that the picture painted by the public-choice school of voters who are primarily motivated by self-interest is a misleading, not to say an inaccurate one?

Probably not all would do so. They would quite likely concede that empirical research had achieved a higher degree of sophistication and had thereby succeeded in avoiding many of the pitfalls that lie in wait for the political scientist who tries to determine whether it is self-interest or public interest that plays the predominant role in voting. They would find it satisfactory that these conclusions are not based solely on observations of the individual's 'behaviour', 'expressions of will', and 'motivations', all of which can be deceptive sources of knowledge about self-interest, and that the respondents have also been required to express 'judgements' about economic changes both in their private lives and in society at large, as well as their 'preferences' by indicating which party they choose. Nevertheless, even intimate information can be unreliable. Not unlike the fox who declared the grapes to be sour, the voter perhaps does not even admit to himself that his economic circumstances have deteriorated; however, this objection might be rebutted by arguing that subjective assessments are more important than objective realities in the theory of economic voting. But the voter might also have simply mistaken what it is the various parties stand for.

In the introductory chapter were listed some of the sources of error that can be encountered in trying to reconstruct the public interest. As we have seen, electoral researchers have opted for a theoretical conception of the public interest that is connected to what was called 'ethical preferences' or 'convictions' of what is best for society as a whole, instead of calculating it through some sort of addition of the personal preferences of individual members of society. Not all have been as careful as Kinder and Kiewiet[62] and checked the correlation between self-interest and public interest to make sure that assessments of the state of the country's economy are not simply generalizations of the respondents' personal situations. Furthermore, to take an example of how the logic of the relation can be inverted in the opposite direction, we have just seen[63] how 'self-interest' could be defined so broadly as 'enlightened self-interest' that it could not be distinguished from 'altruism'.

Despite these objections the philosophers could still make, it is none the less our conclusion that the evidence comes down pretty clearly in support of one of the two hypotheses concerning the motives for voting. In the context of an interview, the respondent can hardly perceive either the request to assess his personal economic situation or the request to assess the way the government runs the economy as particularly vague or incomprehensible. Researchers have provided us with a truly valid measure of self-interest and public interest among voters. The analysis of collected data is also now carried out in such a way that it comes ever closer to meeting the three requirements set out in the beginning of this chapter. Following Kramer's pioneering work of 1971, research on economic voting has to an increasing extent been marked by a 'rationalistic' approach instead of one inspired by the natural sciences. In the majority of studies assessments of personal finances and the national economy are not confounded as they are in the example just mentioned; the question of the nature of the voters' action is left deliberately 'open'. And the demand for 'empirical' evidence, finally, although not complete for all countries, must be said to be very well satisfied. We are, in other words, in a position to come to a conclusion. The extensive empirical material that has been produced through modern research into economic voting makes it impossible to uphold the first assumption of the public-choice school that the voters are primarily guided by self-interest.

3

Are Politicians Vote-Maximizers?

THE CONCEPT OF VOTE-MAXIMIZATION

According to the second assumption of the public-choice school, politicians, just like voters, are primarily guided by their self-interest. Theorists of the school do not contest the obvious fact that politicians *say* that they strive towards the general good. This they must do in order to be re-elected. However, to command the power of government with all its benefits is what the theorists believe to be dearest to the politicians. Politicians try to maximize their votes in order to gain power rather than in order to put their political platforms into practice. How should one go about putting this hypothesis concerning politicians as vote-maximizers to an empirical test?

Downs's clarity and consistency makes him once again a suitable starting-point for a discussion of this problem; the distinction between vote-maximization and the realization of political goals is taken from him. Downs goes directly to the question of how to account for the proliferation of ideological statements in politics if, indeed, the self-interest hypothesis is correct and politicians are 'interested in gaining office *per se*, not in promoting a better or an ideal society'. His answer is that ideologies can help rational citizens by cutting down the amount of time they need to make their choice. By voting according to the general ideological leaning of each party instead of comparing their proposals in detail, the voters can drastically reduce their 'information costs', as Downs puts it. Similarly, the 'decision costs' of a party are much lowered if it does not have to make a precise estimation of the effect various reforms might have on the party's support amongst different groups of voters but rather 'fashions an ideology which it believes will attract the greatest number of votes'.

As anyone in the advertising business can tell you, it is sometimes risky to sum up a message in a simple slogan. According to Downs there is thus a risk that people take ideologies too seriously. They can become more important than the party strategists had planned. Instead of being the means to vote-maximization they are intended to be, ideologies become a goal in their own right.

Parties seek as their final ends the power, income, and prestige that go with office. Ideologies develop out of this desire as means to gaining office. But the maintenance of ideologies may become a subsidiary end with direct rewards in terms of prestige, especially if a change in ideology is regarded by the public as loss of integrity or responsibility. Thus the means to a larger end becomes an end in itself, and its attainment may sometimes conflict with attainment of the larger end. In the real world, this irrational development is a common phenomenon in social organizations.

But the author does not consider this to be a serious objection to the self-interest hypothesis. It is what is true most often that is decisive. According to Downs, ideologies are seldom sustained if they come into conflict with a party's basic interest in gaining office. He does not entertain the slightest doubt that vote-maximization is generally given priority over the realization of political ideals.

As Downs saw it, the weakness of theories that had existed up till then was that political scientists did not have a realistic view of the motives that steer the decisions of a government. The researchers who assumed that citizens tried to attain their personal preferences as consumers or business men seemed to believe in a complete conversion to altruism when these same citizens took up a political role. For this reason the political scientists also failed to capture satisfactorily the function of economic policy in their models. Downs therefore recommended a drastic change in research strategy: he encouraged social scientists to make a systematic survey of government decisions in, for example, the field of economic policy, with the aim of explaining them in the light of the hypothesis that they were taken above all to realize the government's principal goal of being re-elected.[1]

Thus was born the idea from which has developed the modern view that politicians primarily seek to maximize the number of votes they get.

THE POLITICAL BUSINESS CYCLE

It was not until almost twenty years later that Downs's proposal gave rise to any more extensive empirical testing. In the mid-1970s a number of articles began to be published about a phenomenon that was called 'the political business cycle'. If it were true, as Downs maintained, that politicians are first and foremost vote-maximizers, then we should expect the government to try and manipulate the economy in such a way as to make it as attractive as possible at election time and thus make the prospects of the government's being re-elected as favourable as possible. In other words, we should be able to count on the government's stimulating the economy so that the favourable effects would be most noticeable in an election year whereas cuts and other measures with unfavourable consequences would not be taken until after election-day. The electoral tactics of the parties could thus be expected to give rise to fluctuations in economic activity. Instead of acting to mitigate the swing between recession and over-heating, which according to economic theory is an important task for politicians, it was quite likely that the politicians actually created exogenous movements based on their own interests—the political business cycle.

Research into the political business cycle also springs from a second source older than Downs. The term was introduced by Kalecki, a Marxian economist who, independently of Keynes, anticipated many of the latter's conclusions concerning an active economic policy. However, Kalecki did not believe that politicians would really try to even out the business cycle simply because they were capable of doing so. Keynes was a member of the upper class who believed in government by an élite inspired by concern for the public interest. As a Marxist Kalecki was suspicious of such idealism. He assumed that the government mainly served the interests of capital and these did not consist in attaining full employment. Full employment would press up wages and even out differences with respect to income and power. This was hardly a goal desired by private enterprise. On the other hand, the capitalists were not opposed to all economic intervention by government. In times of recession investment grants and other forms of support were welcome. As the economy began to approach full employment, however, the demands put on the government by big business would lead it to cut governmental expenditures and the political business cycle would be a reality.[2]

Considering that the public-choice school with its self-interest hypothesis is usually associated with the right-wing revival of the 1980s, it is interesting to note that one of its central tenets has actually sprung from the left, from Marxism. On further thought, this is perhaps not so remarkable, for Marxism is, like public choice, an interest theory.

The research of the 1970s and 1980s gives only very weak support to the theory of political business cycles if, indeed, one can speak of support at all—this should be made clear right from the beginning. In the survey that follows the reader will meet many instances in which scholars have squeezed their material in an untenable fashion in order to be able to concur with the theory, as well as examples of the majority of studies in which the scholar has simply been obliged to draw the negative conclusion that the notion of the political business cycle should be rejected.

William Nordhaus is the first of the modern scholars who have examined the political business cycle. He takes as his point of departure Downs's principle of vote-maximization: 'parties are assumed to be interested only in election outcomes'. The author himself avers that this postulate is somewhat ambiguous: above all it is uncertain whether it is simply the nearest election or vote-maximization in the long term that the parties are thought to have in mind. Or to put the matter in the terms that were to become common: it is debatable whether politicians really are so myopic. (The penchant for special expressions is apparently just as great amongst those who do research into the political business cycle as amongst those who study economic voting.)

Nordhaus tries to test empirically the view that unemployment should be high at the beginning of a mandate period and decline as an election approaches, after which it should rise again in a recurring cycle. Data from nine countries covering the period from 1947 to 1972 were collected. The results can be read from a table with four lines for each country. In Australia, for example, unemployment rose on three occasions before an election and fell on four, whereas after an election it rose on three occasions and fell on five. Thus in seven instances the Australian data coincided with the theory but in eight the theory was not confirmed. To sum up the results, the data for Australia, Canada,

Japan, and Great Britain did not support the theory, a weak positive correlation was found for France and Sweden, while the theory was corroborated by evidence from three countries—Germany, New Zealand, and the United States. Strangely enough, the author bases his conclusions solely on the latter three countries. He writes that 'it is clear that a political business cycle is a significant factor in the operation of some capitalist democratic economies'. The fact that the opposite was true of the majority of countries studied is not mentioned in the conclusions, which instead are largely devoted to a discussion of conceivable remedies for the political business cycle.[3]

The debate quickly became side-tracked. Scholarly work took up the question of whether voters and politicians are 'myopic' or 'strategic' (whether they think of the next election or of the longer term). In an article with the somewhat misleading title 'A Political Model of the Business Cycle' with data from the four presidential elections between 1957 and 1972, Duncan MacRae states that a direct test of the theory of political business cycles requires that voters are myopic—and furthermore that data is available not only for the state of the economy but also for all other issues of domestic and foreign policy, a gigantic task. An indirect test on the one hand would be to investigate whether politicians *think* that voters are myopic. Instead of giving an answer to the question of the extent to which the incumbent government forms its economic policy with an eye to maximizing its share of the vote, MacRae informs us that the myopia theory best accounts for the policy pursued by the Kennedy and Johnson administrations, whereas the hypothesis of strategic orientation better fits the years under Eisenhower and Nixon.[4]

How far back does the memory of the average voter actually reach? This is a question which has occupied Bruno Frey, who in a number of articles has discussed how one might construct an adequate model of the rationally vote-maximizing government and the rationally critical voter. Given certain assumptions, empirical evidence from the USA, Great Britain, and Germany, and in some cases even from the Scandinavian countries, indicates that governments try to optimize the economy on the eve of an election. However, Frey's main point is that so many factors come into play that it is exceptionally difficult to state anything definite, even with the simplifying assumptions of the model. 'The optimization problem faced by the government as sketched above is so complex that it is in general impossible or at least extremely difficult to derive an analytical solution. The problem is, of course, still more difficult to solve in the real world.' Consequently, he feels he can only provide partial answers to the question of the effect politicians can have on the economy. When the government enjoys popular support, left-wing governments tend to increase taxes and expenditures while right-wing governments tend to reduce them; when the government is afraid of losing the election (however the author is able to determine that with any certainty), it tends, regardless of political leaning, to increase expenditures; political business cycles thus arise only when governments believe that they otherwise stand to lose; but there are in many cases administrative barriers that prevent such cycles from emerging.[5]

In a later study Frey and a collaborating author point out that the government's economic policy is not solely determined by a will to survive but also by ideological considerations; that economic conditions influence government's choice of policy although rather indirectly, as through the budget deficit in Great Britain (but not in the USA); that the government is not alone in deciding economic policy but is also influenced by the administration with its special interests. 'To summarize: Neither the "pure" economists' assumptions that economic variables alone explain government behaviour, nor the assumption that governments maximize votes only seems to be adequate. A satisfactory model of government behaviour and politico-economic interdependence requires that a more complex model be considered.'[6]

The single work that most energetically argues for the existence of a political business cycle is Edward Tufte's much debated book *Political Control of the Economy*; as the reader will recall, this was the study that also argues more forcefully than others for the thesis that voters let their pocket-books decide for them. Tufte maintains that politicians manipulate economic policy with the main aim of getting re-elected. In a style as elegant as it is categorical, he argues that the government controls unemployment and inflation so that they reach their lowest levels at election time and payments from the social security system so that they are at a maximum. The best way to reduce the former figures is, he says, to hold a presidential election; if one wishes the latter to reach their zenith, one has only to wait for the months immediately preceding an election.

Tufte's data have been questioned and it has turned out to be difficult to reproduce his results. However, even if one accepts the validity of his figures, his presentation of them confronts the reader with a number of peculiarities. For example in the first and centrally important table of the book are presented figures showing the way in which disposable incomes have changed in election years and non-election years for twenty-seven democracies between 1961 and 1972. Since election years are less frequent than the others, a relative measure is used to achieve comparability (three of four cases = 75 per cent, two of six cases = 33 per cent, etc.). Tufte believes he is able to claim that in nineteen of the twenty-seven countries incomes increased more rapidly during election years than in other years. That is certainly a trend—but not a particularly strong one. After all, it is not the figure o that would indicate the absence of any correlation (such a result would be an exceptionally strong confirmation of the counter-hypothesis) but rather an even half of the cases examined, i.e. thirteen or fourteen countries. And Tufte's result was nineteen. In his comments, however, he does not touch upon this matter. 'The findings are clear,' he writes. 'Evidence for an electoral-economic cycle was found in 19 of the 27 countries . . . There is, then, an electoral rhythm to the national economic performance of many capitalist democracies.'

This result is thus derived from aggregate, comparative data. Tufte also made a special study of the economic policy of a single country like the United States. For most of the elections between the end of the 1940s and the mid-1970s the theory of political business cycles seemed to find support. But not for the Eisenhower years. How could that be? Perhaps Eisenhower had a different view of what appealed to the voters the most (a balanced budget, for example), something which can give rise to a different cyclical pattern. 'Perhaps there was a political budget cycle. That policy, if it was a policy, may have grown out of a conviction that voters cared as strongly about a balanced federal budget as those who shaped economic policy.' This observation, at once both imaginative and cautious, is quickly transformed in the following paragraph into a categorical conclusion: 'The Eisenhower years demonstrated that when the administration's views on political economy changed the political economic cycle also changed.' No matter which way the data point, Tufte thus claims to find support for his thesis that the politicians manipulate the economy in order to maximize their electoral support on election day. Further from our requirement of openness in empirical testing one cannot go.[7]

With the approach of the 1980s, a change occurred in the debate on the political business cycle. After some years of testing it seemed to be clear that the theory could not be upheld. Researchers ceased trying to save it with more or less artificial devices. They began to reject the theory outright or to reformulate it so completely as to make it almost unrecognizable.

Bennett McCallum adopted a sceptical attitude towards Nordhaus's early study on the political business cycle. It will be recalled that Nordhaus had not found support for his theory in six of the nine countries examined. Of the three in which it was claimed the theory was confirmed, one was the United States. McCallum decided to test Nordhaus's theory against his own quarter-yearly data on unemployment in the United States for the years 1948–74. He did not find any support for the political business cycle theory, however, nor did he believe that the American government had actually attempted to manipulate the economy in the way the theory presupposes.[8]

A Danish researcher has looked into the occurrence of political business cycles in seventeen OECD countries. He selected stable governments that enjoyed parliamentary majorities and thus were in the best position to carry out the manipulation the theory points to. He found no support for the theory. Not even those governments which had the greatest conceivable opportunity to exercise control commanded the economy to the extent required by the theory. Nor did the economy change during mandate periods in the fashion the theory presupposes. 'In addition to this somewhat negative conclusion we should add another. It was not possible, as expected, to find an election-year effect in the data. In none of the diagrams drawn does the last year stand out as the most expansionary, or otherwise as the "best".' A certain pattern did emerge (with the greatest amount of expansion during the second year and the greatest amount of inflation in the third, probably related to the need to fulfil election promises)— but one quite different from that described by the political business cycle.[9]

In an extensive follow-up the author encountered considerable difficulties in trying to reproduce the results that supported the theory, results that were first published in Nordhaus's article; Tufte's results could not be found at all in the author's own data. The political business cycle appeared to be 'all wrong'. The author was able to demonstrate the existence of a pattern lasting a mandate period but a pattern quite different from the one predicted, one caused by promised reforms. Far from being the selfish and rational manipulators of the economy, the politicians appeared to be rather helpless victims of their own election promises.[10]

In an extensive British research programme concerning political economy it has not been possible to confirm the political business cycle theory. The empirical results can be interpreted in far too many ways. Does the absence of a political business cycle depend on the fact that the government has not attempted to act as expected or that it has tried and failed? Does the absence of any reaction on the part of the voters indicate that they are myopic or, on the contrary, that they are far-sighted? 'It is difficult to accept a model which sometimes works and sometimes does not.' Testing the theory led to conclusions which lent less support to the view that politicians manipulate the economy than to the view that the voters set limits to the formation of economic policy.[11] An attempt to reproduce Tufte's results concerning politically determined payments from the welfare system raised doubts that a comparable phenomenon exists in Great Britain.[12]

Reiner Dinkel has carried out comprehensive analyses of economic policy in the United States and Germany. He has not found anything to support the political business cycle theory. 'Despite popular belief to the contrary, we could find no conclusive evidence of a political business cycle in Germany or the United States.' There were plenty of reasons why governments should not give in to such temptations. The voters would not like it, for they dislike the budget deficits that are the inevitable result; if all parties acted in this way, the voters would look for new parties; in coalition governments the largest party would receive the severest punishment; no government has anything to win from an economy in chaos.

Summarizing our findings, theoretically a government may increase its re-election chances by initiating a cyclical economic policy. But our research did not establish that the German or U.S. governments have in fact acted that way. Such a result, at first glance, appears surprising. But there are many factors discouraging governments from creating a political business cycle even though such a policy might be successful.[13]

Donald Wittman has criticized the Downsian concept of politicians. Two models were compared: in the first, candidates had policy preferences as well as an interest in winning *per se*; in the second, candidates were interested only in winning. Testable propositions were derived via the use of comparative statistics. The results of recent studies were shown to be consistent with the synthesis model but not with the pure Downsian model.[14]

Another research team tested American data to see if unemployment followed political changes. It discovered some co-variation but in comparison with the average increase in the number of job openings the changes in unemployment were not large and the political business cycle not especially conspicuous.[15]

In a very broadly cast survey of the literature published in 1986, the author writes as follows about the political business cycle theory: 'The empirical support for the theory is often weak . . . The more it has been tested, the greater have become the number of objections raised against it, however. It has been difficult to demonstrate the existence of any cycles in the empirical studies.'[16]

Another scholar has analysed the economic policy of the United States, Great Britain, and Germany. His conclusion is that the government's policy is more affected by 'shocks' that hit the economy. Furthermore, there are so many errors in attempts to achieve popularity with the help of changes in unemployment and inflation that the whole notion of trying to plan these changes rationally in order to maximize votes appears ridiculous.

These results imply that an incumbent administration is not in a position to manipulate the economy for political purposes, even supposing it could manage the economy in this way. Since the popularity series is dominated by "shocks", then any strategy designed to increase public support by manipulating the economy prior to an election could easily be thwarted by unexpected circumstances. Thus one of the main links in the political business cycle, the link between the economy and popularity is too weak and unstable to sustain the thesis that governments can manipulate the economy for political gain.

And his conclusion is categorical: 'The present discussion leads to the clear conclusion that a political business cycle . . . does not exist. Political popularity is not as responsive to changes in the economy as many writers have supposed.'[17]

The political business cycle theory has thus been rejected in an increasing number of studies. In others it has come to be reformulated. For example, a pair of scholars attacked the vision held by the public-choice school of naïve voters who are helpless victims of unscrupulous, vote-maximizing politicians. They presume instead that the voters are more 'sophisticated' and judge the politicians solely in terms of their responsibilities. The voters do not punish a president for inflation caused by his predecessor, for example, nor do they reward him for an expansive policy if it leads to higher rates of inflation in the future. Without letting themselves be duped, the voters make their assessments on the basis of changes in real national income. These scholars have put forward empirical evidence showing that their view of the sophisticated voter comes closer to reality than the description of the public-choice school of easily deceived and myopic voters. Their conclusion was that the public-choice theories 'are not so much undermined as in need of minor refinement'.[18]

Now it might be questioned whether such a minor refinement is sufficient. In actual fact, voters who do not allow themselves to be manipulated by short-sighted, vote-maximizing politicians and who judge the latter according to what they accomplish over time for the best of society seem to be the direct opposite of those envisaged by the theory of political business cycles. Voters like these, as well as the politicians to whom they give their support, are characterized by what we in our broader perspective call solicitude for the public interest instead of self-interest.

In certain studies purely theoretical analyses of discrepancies in the theory of political business cycles have been carried out. Regardless of the outcome of the empirical tests of the theory, would the cycle be broken (as has sometimes been claimed in the public-choice literature) if the voters became better informed and thereby more difficult to hoodwink by selfish, opportunistic politicians? This is not so certain. The electorate comprises several generations, each with its own interests and temporal horizon. It is conceivable that politicians could play these different interests off against each other so that a cycle was put in motion, even if the voters were perfectly informed.[19]

Other scholars have devoted their attention to other sub-groups of the electorate besides generations—social classes, for example. The problem has been this. A contradiction seemed to exist between the two assumptions of the public-choice school: if the voters were rational, they should after all be able to see through the attempts of the politicians to manipulate the economy. However, the parties recruit voters from different social groups with divergent interests, the adherents of the public-choice school have pointed out. The variety of interests can make it so difficult to take stock of political events that governments can devote themselves to vote-maximization without it being all too obvious to the voters.[20]

A large Canadian study also looked into the question of the political business cycle. As was mentioned in Chapter 2, the Canadian voters behave in a surprising fashion: the worse the economy, the greater their support for the incumbent government. The political business cycle theory was dismissed. 'On balance, the now-classic formulation of the political business cycle finds little support in Canadian attitudinal data.'[21]

Finally, when it comes to Scandinavia, a few special studies of the political business cycle have been made. It has been difficult to find support for the theory. One scholar finds 'only the most tenuous evidence' in the case of Norway and 'no evidence whatsoever' for Sweden.[22]

In several penetrating studies Johan Lybeck has attempted to prove the existence of a political business cycle in Sweden. His conclusions 'must be rather discouraging for those who believe in a systematic interplay between economic and political factors'. The governments have not 'tried to steer the economy so that it will be in the best possible position before an election'. The single exception to this is the minority government run by the Liberals in the spring of 1979, when expenditures increased rapidly prior to the election in September. His conclusion is: 'Thus there does not exist any evidence for a permanent political business cycle in Sweden.'[23]

Focusing on the past fifteen years, Lars Jonung in 1985 also stated that a political business cycle could not be found in Sweden. This does not necessarily mean that the government has not tried to bring one about. But in a country as dependent upon international markets as Sweden, this is not so easy to do. Whether or not the government has tried to steer the economy in order to maximize its votes, there is no empirical evidence to support the view that it has actually engaged in such manipulation.[24]

VOTE-MAXIMIZATION AND SOCIALISM

The question of whether politicians are vote-maximizers has also been examined in another way. A pair of American researchers recently put forward the more limited question about the motives that direct the actions of socialist leaders: 'Are socialist leaders vote-maximizers?' Considering how rich the European data for party and electoral studies are, it was high time to use this material to test the view of the celebrated public-choice school concerning the dominant role of self-interest in politics.

The researchers were led to examine this question by the observation that the socialist parties have never had a majority among the electorate. When the popular vote was broadened at the turn of the century to give an ever greater share of the European working class the franchise, the arguments for a revolutionary upheaval were weakened. Hopes were set on winning political power through peaceful means. But the socialist parties' share of the electorate remained just below the magical 50 per cent limit everywhere; according to the authors, this is to be simply explained by the fact that the working class, despite its own expectations, never came to constitute a majority of the population —in later decades its relative size in fact declined. The possibility of increasing their number of votes by appealing to other social groups then presented itself to the socialist parties. Michels made this reflection as early as 1915, and since his days it has been commonplace to assert that the socialist parties would do better in elections if they tried to gain support from the middle class.

By examining statistics on social groups and voting from seven countries—Belgium, Denmark, Finland, France, Norway, Sweden, and Germany—the authors have shown that the matter is more complicated than this. The leaders of the socialists are confronted with a dilemma, for the workers become less apt to vote for them if the party collects votes from other social groups. In relation to the problem of vote-maximization, it is thus a question of making an optimum trade-off between the largest possible gains from the middle class and the least possible losses from the workers.

Faithful to their rationalistic credo, the authors emphasize that the task of social science is not limited to analysing what has actually happened. Conceivable alternatives should be studied as well and the politicians' choice between various possibilities should be explained. 'A theory must rediscover opportunities that were lost, possibilities that were inherent at each junction, and alternatives that remain open.' In this spirit the authors reconstructed the different electoral strategies that stood open to the socialist leaders: the 'class strategy', the 'completely classless strategy', and a more 'limited classless strategy'. Their research question was put as follows: 'Are socialist leaders vote maximizers? Or are they driven by an autonomous concern with class, a concern that restricts their willingness to compete for votes? And if they did not seek to maximize the socialist share of the electorate, how costly was it to their electoral performance?'

The result was that the vote-maximization hypothesis was discarded straight away. None of the parties examined was characterized by vote-maximization. The Scandinavian Social Democrats, successful as they were, would have had much more to gain had they tried to increase their votes from the middle class. For example, if one bases one's calculations on the class structure of 1970, the Danish Social Democrats would have been able to recruit and keep the largest possible number of voters if the share of workers had been 41 per cent instead of 72.5 per cent as was in fact the case; for Norway the comparable figures are 29 and 47 per cent, respectively, for Sweden 21 and 78 per cent. Concern for other values (class, ideology, relations with the trade union movement) has outweighed the desire for votes. The French, Finnish, and German Social Democrats had, prior to 1933, an even more difficult situation. The 'completely classless strategy' would have been the best one with regard to vote-maximization, with the 'class strategy' coming second and the 'limited classless strategy' last. The parties vacillated between these alternatives. Up until 1970, for example, the French Socialists seemed to choose almost the worst possible strategy. They tried to win middle-class votes without losing any workers but failed on both counts. The German left landed half-way between the next worst strategy, which in this case would have been an unqualified bid for the working-class vote, and the worst strategy, which was a half-hearted appeal to the middle class.

The authors formed their conclusions into a powerful polemic against Downs and the vote-maximization theorem. Parties cannot jump freely from one position to another in order to adopt the policy they believe the majority of voters accepts at any one time. To disregard such limitations on the parties' room to manœuvre is to commit the error of reducing the analysis of political science to 'empty formalism'. Downs and his followers have conjured up a strange world in which votes alone are worth anything, but in real life parties also struggle to achieve other goals. Equally 'absurd' is the conception of these theoreticians that the views held by the electorate are independent of the parties and something to which the politicians are obliged to accommodate themselves. On the contrary, it is the politicians who 'present the public with images of society, evoke collective identifications, instill political commitments' and thereby create opinion.[25]

CONCLUSIONS

The conclusion of this chapter is that the self-interest hypothesis cannot be sustained with regard to politicians either. The basis for this judgement is first and foremost the extensive research that might be gathered under the heading of 'the political business cycle'. The analysis of the electoral strategies of European socialists, referred to above, points in the same direction. Now it is true that 'vote-maximization' is a broader concept, but if one aims to discuss the latter with the help of empirical findings, the studies mentioned are the closest thing at hand. There is moreover a remarkable similarity between studies of the 'political business cycle' and of 'economic voting'. Both of these themes are the object of highly integrated debates on which the international scientific community has focused its interest.

If we return to the three criteria set out at the beginning of our quest, we can first assert that most of the scholars in both fields, economic voting as well as the political business cycle, work with rational models. The voters in the one field, the politicians in the other, are expressly considered to be actors who plan and evaluate, and who act with the conscious intent to satisfy their preferences. Secondly, the academic debate in both fields is often open-ended in the way it tests hypotheses. From a methodological point of view, the debate on economic voting seems however to have the edge since a counterhypothesis—the sociotropic hypothesis *versus* the pocket-book hypothesis—has been formulated and tested. In research on the political business cycle the self-interest hypothesis alone has been made operational while its opposite, programme implementation, has (quite naturally) been more difficult to test in a stringent fashion, unless one is to carry out the immense descriptive task of mapping out policy decisions in detail. When it comes to empirical facts, finally, both areas of research have produced overwhelming amounts of data. Completely unambiguous they are not. Granted, one can on purely theoretical grounds imagine that many governments have tried to manipulate the economy for tactical gains at elections but constantly failed. Nevertheless, the facts indicate overwhelmingly, if not conclusively, that the image of the politician who is primarily a vote-maximizer has as little empirical support as the view of the voter who votes on the basis of his pocket-book.

4

Are Bureaucrats Budget-Maximizers?

Even if bureaucrats carry out the wishes of the voters and the decisions of politicians by performing various sorts of tasks, it is, according to the third assumption of the public-choice school, their self-interest that best accounts for their actions. It is not a will to be the loyal servant that leads bureaucrats constantly to expand their administration but rather, it is claimed, an ambition to improve their salaries and other perquisites. What has lent this idea certain credence is of course the rapid expansion of the public sector in the last few decades. Everyone knows that the number of bureaucrats has increased again and again. In many quarters this development is regarded as a serious strain on the political system with the consequence that the political debate during the 1980s has come to be characterized by cries for budget cuts and a general critique of bureaucracy.

To accept the self-interest hypothesis on the evidence of such administrative expansion is however to buy a pig in a poke. Before jumping to conclusions one should look to see if there are not other explanations of the growth of the public sector. In this chapter the hypothesis that the growth of bureaucracy is best explained by the self-interest of the bureaucrats will be critically examined.

As was mentioned in Chapter 1, the hypothesis has been formulated by such leading members of the public-choice school as Tullock, Downs, and Niskanen. The latter's study *Bureaucracy and Representative Government* (1971) has come to be the most renowned and will be taken here to represent the position of the public-choice school regarding the third level—bureaucracy—in our analysis of self-interest and public interest in Western politics.

Economists have developed a demand model to depict consumer

behaviour on the market and a supply model to depict the profit-oriented firm. Niskanen wished to put forward a similar supply model for politics. What corresponded closest to the productive, privately owned firm operating in the economic market was, in his view, the bureaucracy. He called his object of analysis a 'bureau' and defined it as an organization whose owner and staff cannot appropriate the difference between income and expenditures to themselves as personal income, and the revenues of which come at least in part from some other source than the sale of goods and services. Instead a bureau is financed through grants from politicians, the sponsoring organization, in exchange for an undertaking to carry out a certain activity and thereby achieve certain expected results.

The very conception of politics as an offer made by the bureaucrats to the public and elected representatives reflects the view that the bureaucracy holds the initiative in moving developments forward. The 'sponsoring organization' is given a remarkable passive role to play in Niskanen's model. The reason for this was partly that he considered the politicians to be completely under the control of the bureaucrats. Since the distinguishing feature of state administration is the absence of competition, the bureaucrats have an advantage through their monopoly over knowledge. The politicians in the 'control committees' that analyse budget proposals are not really in any position to question the estimates of the bureaucracy, not least because these committees (in accordance with the sectorization and segmentation of politics, which political scientists were later to write so much about) are dominated by the very politicians who have the greatest interest in, and the greatest demand for, the activity in question.

Niskanen concentrates his attention on the head of each administration. This person is presumed to maximize utility. It was for Niskanen a matter of methodological principle to follow the canons of rationalism and construct a model based on the motives of individuals and not, as had been the case in much previous research, on some organic theory of the state *à la* Confucius, Plato, Max Weber, or Woodrow Wilson, which presents the administration as a collective idealization that should serve the public interest in a particular fashion. Since the bureaucrats themselves do not receive any economic advantage from greater efficiency or larger surpluses, the only way they can stand to make a personal gain is to see to it that their own administration grows and thereby, according to the practice Niskanen attributes to state administration, the salaries and other benefits of its employees as well. Budget-maximization is an instinct in every forward-looking bureaucrat. An increase in the budget is often the solution to any internal problem within a bureaucracy. In competitive industry it is sufficient that a single firm is a profit-maximizer for all the rest to adopt the same strategy. Within bureaucracy it is the other way round.

In contrast, in a bureaucratic environment, one person who serves his personal interests or a different perception of public interest is often sufficient to prevent others from serving their perception of the public interest. It is *impossible* for any one bureaucrat to act in the public interest, because of the limits on his information and the conflicting interests of others, regardless of his personal motivations. This leads even the most selfless bureaucrats to choose some feasible, lower-level goal . . . A bureaucrat who may not be personally motivated to maximize the budget of his bureau is usually driven by conditions both internal and external to the bureau to do just that.

What makes it possible to maximize the budget is the basic difference between allocating resources via a bureaucracy and via a market. While bureaucracy maximizes its budget, the market maximizes the difference between total utility and total cost. There is no place in a bureaucracy for marginal cost analysis and the political sponsor therefore never knows what the marginal gain of an additional unit of resource would be. As a result, the bureaucracy is always too large, in fact twice as large, Niskanen maintains, as it ought to be, and is always the source of a waste of resources.

Niskanen tries to lend credence to his argument with a counter-example. What would happen to a civil servant who was able to show that the present activity of the bureaucracy could be carried out within a considerably smaller budget? In a profit-oriented enterprise he would be rewarded with a bonus, promotion, and the opportunity to pursue work on his idea. If he did not succeed, it would always be open to him to move to one of the competitors with his freshly won knowledge. In a state bureaucracy he might possibly receive a mention, perhaps be transferred without a raise, but above all he would win the disapproval of his colleagues and the suspicion of the new employees.

Niskanen wrote his book with memories of his experiences as an administrator in the American Department of Defense, to which he had come full of high hopes with McNamara during the Kennedy era, fresh in his mind. He presents his thesis with mathematical stringency, showing with various supply curves how the political system is constantly pressed to adjust itself to excessive budgets for the bureaucracy. His clarity, elegance, and, not least of all, his daring attracted much academic attention and his book has come to be one of the most cited in modern social science.

Niskanen concludes his book with a call for steps to be taken to check the swelling bureaucracy. The advantage the bureaucracy has over its political sponsors should been broken by introducing competition within the state apparatus and privatizing certain operations.[1]

THE BUDGETARY PROCESS

The budget-maximization hypothesis has not been made the object of tests as coherent and systematic as those applied to the hypotheses concerning pocket-book voting and the political business cycle. Niskanen's model seems to arouse a strange combination of admiration and indifference in political scientists, for it is not uncommon to hear them say that they are impressed by the formal presentation of the book; yet they apparently feel no inspiration to test the validity of his hypothesis against empirical data. At times it is even claimed that Niskanen's model cannot be tested, a point to which we shall return at the end of this chapter. Furthermore, those articles which do deal with his model have a strongly theoretical bent. Niskanen's formulae and supply curves are marched up one page and down the next, after which the article is usually concluded with some particular case that seems to have been chosen to confirm the author's thesis. Such literature can easily arouse a sense of disappointment in a person who sets empiricism as one of his guiding lights and, as author after author just accepts the model, tries to find out if the hypothesis stands up in reality.

Most of the studies that have been made of Niskanen's model have moreover been inspired by a second tradition within research on administration, one which originated at about the same time as Niskanen's book was written. In the large-scale investigations of Aaron Wildavsky, Thomas Anton, and Hugh Heclo we can read about what actually happens when bureaucrats and politicians interact in the budgetary process. Contacts between these groups are intensive—and the more intensive they are, the less difficulty the bureaucrats seem to have in getting things their own way. The principle is confidence and co-operation. It is important to keep the politicians informed from as early a stage in the process as possible. To hide costs or let them increase in an unplanned fashion is self-defeating; there is nothing politicians hate more than to feel deceived. The demands for increases from the bureaucrats are haggled over by the politicians in an almost ritualistic pattern. The administrative units know that many of their demands are unrealistically high but it is important to get into line for the next hand-out. The politicians devote themselves to paring the budget not only on objective grounds but also from a need to show the voters that they treat the finances of the state with care and responsibility. The budgetary process is characteristically incremental in nature: the amounts allotted one year form the basis for the following year's budget and discussions focus on adjustments at the margin. But no matter how this game is played or what arguments pass between bureaucrats and politicians, the public sector seems to grow by a couple of per cent every year.[2]

In the studies we shall consider the theoretical perspective of Niskanen and other public-choice scholars are combined with the more empirical methodology of budgetary process analysis. Four small auxiliary verbs facilitate our survey of this debate: we shall ask namely whether bureaucrats actually 'may', 'can', 'dare', and 'want to' devote themselves to budget-maximizing.

When we wonder if they *may* do so, it is not any legal authority we have in mind—such a rule would seem absurd—but rather whether it is the case that bureaucrats are actually given an opportunity by the politicians to maximize budgets without interference. This question brings us directly to the main objection levelled at Niskanen's model. The passive role assigned the politicians by Niskanen is considered by the empirical researchers to give an utterly unrealistic picture of the budgetary process. If one wishes to view politics from the supply side, it would be more telling, the critics claim, to cast the party politicians as the entrepreneurs of public service. It is the programmes of the parties that are offered to the voters and then, depending upon the voters' choice, implemented by the bureaucracy, for which the threat of a cut in allocations is as alive as the prospects of budget-maximization.

Do the politicians really permit the bureaucrats to increase their expenditures unchecked? No, answers Robert Goodin: keeping allocations to the bureaucracy under control is one of the tasks the politicians devote most energy to. Goodin examined the American budgetary process and found that Congress had tightened its grip on budget matters. Between 1969 and 1976, for example, the number of hearings dealing with this increased by 74 per cent in the House of Representatives and by 55 per cent in the Senate. A sceptic might object that such figures are at most an indication of change; it is after all conceivable that these hearings are a sign of the opposite—that the politicians truly feel themselves boxed into a corner and take such steps for that reason. According to Goodin, an analysis of the demand side of politics does not support Niskanen's hypothesis either. Committees that increased costs had gradually lost power to budget committees placed over them. President Reagan's slaughter of the budget was a good example of the way in which politicians could assert themselves against the bureaucrats. Goodin is also dubious about Niskanen's suggestion of strengthening the politicians by letting the bureaucrats compete with each other. Studies of American defence policy indicate that, on the contrary, if two bureaucracies find themselves in a conflict of interest, they prefer to enter a secret agreement than to weaken each other in front of the politicians. They also showed that the motives of politicians and bureaucrats can be the reverse of what Niskanen presumes: a politician could want to expand a programme while a bureaucrat suggests cuts be made in it.

Niskanen's model of the interactions between rational vote-maximizing politicians and rational budget-maximizing bureaucrats is flatly wrong. It is wrong in suggesting that information-manipulation on the supply side will necessarily go unchecked, and in supposing that the demand side will necessarily be dominated by politicians with unusually strong desires for the goods in question. Niskanen's model is also wrong in supposing that bureaucrats will necessarily compete if their interests are in conflict, and it is wrong in attributing the motivations it does to actors on both sides of the bargaining game. Consequently, and inevitably, Niskanen is wrong in his conclusion that bureaucratic goods and services are oversupplied (or overpriced) by something up to a factor of two.[3]

In *The Economic Theory of Representative Government* Albert Breton discusses Niskanen's notion that political life is a question of developing and selling goods and services produced in the public sector. To Breton it is obvious that this task is performed primarily by the politicians, not the bureaucrats. He would like to modify not only Niskanen's model but also Downs's. Competition between parties for votes is certainly an important prerequisite for party operation. But such competition does not occur only every second or third or fourth year. What is more important is the constant competition between parties to see which comes up with the best ideas for political action in different fields. It is this competition that constitutes the most important limitation on the behaviour of the politicians. When dealing with the supply side of politics, one should focus on the politicians, not on the bureaucrats.[4]

In a later article highly critical of Niskanen, Breton, together with a co-author, notes that the military escalation of the war in Vietnam is often cited as the most devastating example of bureaucratic budget-maximization, an idea Niskanen himself touches upon in his book. Memoranda that have subsequently become available to researchers indicate, however, that this conception is quite simply wrong. The politicians did not cave in at all to the budgetary demands of the military. President Johnson's administration had successfully kept the requests of the military in check and had foreseen with surprising accuracy the consequences of various measures to reinforce the troops. The very large military venture that was nevertheless launched was entirely the result of the assessments of the politicians. Thus not even with regard to perhaps the greatest increase of any budgetary item in modern times has it been possible to prove the thesis of budget-maximization. The politicians were able to hold their own line with the help of the instruments of control they had at their disposal.[5]

Miller and Moe also argue that the most serious shortcoming of Niskanen's model is that it blames budget-maximizing bureaucrats for the expansion of the public sector and forgets about the politicians who decide on the requisite financing. They have put forward an alternative model, to which researchers have often returned, and by which it is possible to determine with less prejudice the importance of various groups for increases in expenditures. With the help of this model the problems of large bureaucracies come 'to look very different from those stressed by Niskanen and other critics. In particular, the model implies that their negative assessments of bureaucracy are overdrawn, that their proposals for privatization and competition are often ill-advised, and that the legislature, not the bureaucracy, is primarily to blame for the problems of big government.'[6]

Is it not an inconsistency in Niskanen's thesis, Bruce Benson asks, that the bureaucrats get away with producing something less efficiently than representative politicians would permit? How can it be that such operations are allowed to continue? The answer he develops from an observation made by Niskanen himself: politicians have an interest in dividing themselves up into committees and specializing in those questions they are most concerned about. Even within the framework of a self-interest theory he thereby oversteps the more limited hypothesis regarding budget-maximizing bureaucrats and, without drawing attention to the fact, points to the motives of the politicians as decisive explanatory factors.[7]

If it is true that the bureaucracy controls the development of the public sector, then large and powerful bureaucracies should manage to avoid budget cuts more easily than others. An English scholar has put this hypothesis to a statistical test by examining local government in Thatcher's Britain while controlling for local party politics, centrally earmarked allocations, and variables relating to local conditions. His findings fail to confirm the theory. The bureaucracy does not have the influence presupposed by the advocates of the maximization hypothesis.[8]

There are two fundamental errors in Niskanen's model, writes as authoritative a scholar as Richard Rose in summing up his assessment of Western politics during the 1980s, *Understanding Big Government*. The first is to believe that bureaucracies are allowed to grow in just any fashion without the politicians' being able to do anything about it. The other is to believe that bureaucracies actually wish to grow; we shall return to his argument on this point. Concerning the first, Rose points out that empirical studies of the budgetary process have shown that politicians are actually in a position to control developments. Despite its stringency, the budget-maximization hypothesis amounts to no more than an expression of astonishing simplification and coarse ignorance. It leaves aside 'the constraints that institutions impose upon individuals who hold office within them, and the constraints that the expectations of society place upon the individual pursuit of overt self-interest. In fact, neither politicians nor bureaucrats can do whatever they wish.'[9]

The same opinion is expressed by Peter Self in a basic textbook. To believe that bureaucrats always or even often get their own way misrepresents the restraining and decisive role of politicians in determining allocations to public authorities.[10]

As the years have passed, researchers have thus become more and more convinced that Niskanen assigns politicians an altogether too passive role in the budgetary process. A recently published anthology by Jan-Erik Lane provides a good account of the state of research in Western Europe. Amongst the contributors is a Scandinavian who rejects Niskanen's thesis that it is the bureaucracy that causes the bureaucracy to swell, and an Englishman who, after extensive analyses of the British bureaucracy, says that although the bureaucracy is certainly not without guilt for the expansion of the public sector, this can better be accounted for by the specific political decisions that preceded the expansion. It is the politicians, not the bureaucrats, who are the main actors in the game of politics as the producer of services and activities.[11]

This does not mean, of course, that it is impossible to find bureaucracies that are wasteful or have an unnecessarily large budget. One or two years after Niskanen's book was published, a number of members of the public-choice school led by James Buchanan held a series of seminars on the role of the bureaucracy in the growth of public expenditures. The budget-maximization hypothesis runs all through the articles, a few of which are empirical. One researcher is able to show, for example, that in comparing the private and public provision of services, costs for the former are lower regarding airline service, garbage collection, medical care, fire protection, and electricity supply.[12] A second contributor describes how teachers' salaries are set primarily in relation to their academic education while the results of the pupils are unrelated to the formal qualifications of their teachers: they do just as well when instructed by less qualified teachers. In other words, education is purchased inefficiently.[13] A third compares state universities with private ones and finds that the former have a considerably larger administration.[14]

But even in this circle of orthodox public-choice theoreticians some seeds of doubt were sown. In order to assess the budget-maximization hypothesis, an alternative model with passive bureaucrats was put forward for comparison. The result was that it also predicted that the public sector would expand at an accelerating rate because of the quickly rising production costs in that sector.[15] Moreover, a study comparing two explanations of public-sector growth, one derived from Stigler's theories (presented in Chapter 2) in terms of public interest, the other based on the assumption that bureaucrats act in their own self-interest, ended in a draw.[16]

A decade later another scholar looked around for different types of irresponsible bureaucratic behaviour. After having made the customary criticism of Niskanen for having posited far too powerful bureaucrats, he is able to point to an instance that corresponds fairly closely to Niskanen's view. The case involved the offer of cheap meals to the elderly in Miami. It turns out that it was not the most needy who were the most important clients for the authorities; it was rather they who provided the bureaucrats with an opportunity to get rid of their reserves.[17]

Other researchers have reported how civil servants in the department of public works in France tried to thwart the amalgamation of their department with the department of housing at the end of the 1960s in order to exploit the reform to gain money, power, and prestige for themselves.[18] And Elinor Ostrom has contributed to the literature on Niskanen by showing that increased competition in the field of garbage collection in American cities leads to lower costs.[19]

Turning to the second of our questions, we can note that scholars doubt that bureaucrats *can* maximize their budgets. Niskanen contended that bureaucrats have this potential because in most cases the government authorities have a monopoly in their field and the politicians therefore have no one else to turn to for information. The critics maintain that this is a misunderstanding of the way in which the budgetary process is actually carried out in at least three different respects.

In the first place, bureaucracies often compete with each other in the real world. In the United States the competition between different agencies for the task of running some public services is often very keen.[20]

In the second place, one must not confound competition in market terms with competition within an administration, an error made by the public-choice school. In market competition different firms compete to sell the same goods. As just mentioned, such a situation can also occur within the state administration, but a characteristic feature of bureaucracy is otherwise the competition between agencies to be able to carry out different activities, all of which are financed by the same tax revenues. When the politicians weigh these various activities against each other in order to channel money into projects that will lead to the greatest increase in welfare for the citizens, the bureaucracies actually compete under conditions as severe as those for competing firms.

The notion of a bureau as a single and independent monopolist becomes rather strange, since it might be expected that the many bureaux are competing for as large as possible a part of the total budget of the ministry. In this way there arises a picture which is quite different from that of the bureau as a monopolist, as sketched by Niskanen.[21]

In the third place, it is not certain that the authorities can maximize their own budget even if they should find themselves in a monopoly position. A distinguishing feature of bureaucracies is that they carry heavy costs for 'special resources', something that makes them less flexible than firms on the open market. These special resources can include both manpower and capital. That expertise is the hallmark of bureaucracy is a notion going back at least to Weber. The positions of higher civil servants are usually more secure than those of business executives and their specialization narrows the range of alternative employment for them. Large-scale operations within the state administration, such as the postal and telephone services or the manufacture of military aircraft, must be run at full capacity; nothing is to be gained by letting them go at half-speed. If one examines the state administration concretely, one discovers that the room for maximization or other manipulation of the budget is far less than what Niskanen seems to believe.[22]

In addition, it is pointed out, budget-maximization is a risky business. It entails after all that the bureaucrats break that very rule which researchers have found to be the most important of all in contacts with politicians in the budgetary process: to behave credibly and loyally towards the political sponsors. Do bureaucrats *dare* put this confidence into jeopardy? 'Bureaucrats must keep their lies down to believable proportions or else it will be worth the while of budget reviewers to invest some resources and catch them at their lies.' The margin for him who would inflate his budget is rather small.[23]

Attempts to maximize the budget destroy confidence. ' "Disbelief", notice, is a counter-strategy you can play against a liar even if you do not know the truth yourself. You know enough to discount his reports, at least.' In the American budgetary process, if bureaucrats go beyond what is expected of them, they run a great risk of being hit by a real slash in their budgets. Local politicians in Norway have demonstrated that they are prepared to make drastic budget cuts if they believe that the figures of the bureaucrats are inflated.[24]

Finally, a large part of the debate concerns whether bureaucrats actually *want* to spend time on maximizing the budget. Other motives seem to play a greater role in their actions.

The prospect for promotion ranks very high on the bureaucrat's scale of values. Indeed, budget-maximization is seen by public choice theoreticians as a means to advancement; if the bureau expands, the chances for improvements in wages and other benefits also increase. Where Niskanen errs in this argument, his critics maintain, is in adopting an altogether too hierarchical view of Western European administration. In Great Britain, for example, there are 800 top civil servants within forty-seven departments, all of whom are able to exercise great influence. And under them there are in turn thousands of civil servants. It is in the interaction between these levels that a budget comes into being. In this process the upper and lower civil servants often have widely divergent motives. The lower bureaucrats, who would have most to gain if the bureau grew and offered them greater career opportunities, know that they have slight influence and therefore seek advancement in some other fashion than by arguing for budget-maximization: in the literature on administration, 'doing a good job' is a constantly recurring answer from lower civil servants eager for promotion. By contrast, the top civil servants, who have greater influence on the budget, see little personal gain to be had through budget-maximization but higher risks with such a strategy. At the same time, they are more interested in such immaterial rewards as status and influence, which in fact do not reflect the size of the budget as Niskanen assumes—more on this point below—and for this reason they are not particularly inclined towards budget-maximization either.[25] Niskanen, who claims that his conception of human beings is so much more realistic than the idealized image found in administrative research in the Weberian tradition, of bureaucrats as devoted to the public interest as the Prussian officers were loyal to the Kaiser, is thus himself guilty of a Weberian idealization when he describes the bureaucracy as strictly hierarchical with all power gathered in the hands of the supposedly budget-maximizing top civil servants.

Bureaucrats wish to advance. To do a good job is a more obvious strategy than to attempt something as speculative as maximizing the budget. In fact, the direct opposite, budget-minimization, can be a good method of showing that one is effective and is worthy of a higher post. If the motives of bureaucrats are to be understood, it is necessary to learn their long-term aspirations and not devote undue attention to each particular fiscal year. A bureaucrat can discover 'that the surest way to advancement is the minimization of his bureau's budget, a possible objective of his political superiors'.[26] Secretary of Defense James Schlesinger can be mentioned as one example. He made his career by greatly reducing the budget of the CIA while he was its head.[27] And Caspar Weinberger, another Secretary of Defense, won both his advancement and his nickname 'the knife' from the years he spent successfully slashing budgets at the Department of Health and

Welfare. This fact is pointed out by an author who also tells of the dentist who became energy minister with the express aim of closing down the department and returning to his practice.[28]

To believe that bureaucrats seek to maximize their budgets is also to overestimate their desire to tie their fate to that of their bureau. Transferring from one bureau to another is a common way of making a career, especially in Western Europe. Just as Niskanen under-estimates the competition that actually exists in the American budgetary process, he ignores the mobility that can be found in the more monopolistic administrations of Europe.[29] However, the figures on mobility in American administration are also high: in 1959, 63 per cent of the leading bureaucrats had been employed in more than one administrative agency, and in 1974, 55 per cent had worked as the head of two or more organizations.[30]

The empirically oriented scientists interested in public administration usually point to another strategy that the top bureaucrats seem to prefer to budget-maximization. It is called 'bureau-shaping', and it entails a re-organization so that they can take care of the most interesting tasks themselves. As was noted above, large budgets do not always give the head bureaucrat more prestige and influence. Increases in the payments made by large welfare administrations, for example, hardly affect the head officer. What might tempt him, on the other hand, would be a move from the front line to the planning staff, often to small, centrally placed offices near the finance department with the opportunities they offer for power and control. Such is the situation within the civil service in Canada, where, moreover, the heads of smaller but strategically located offices are better paid than the heads of the large health and social insurance administrations.[31]

'Bureau-shaping' also casts a critical light on Niskanen's recom-mendation to privatize parts of the administration in order to keep a tight rein on budget-maximization. If Niskanen is right, the bureaucrats should oppose privatization. But in Reagan's USA and Thatcher's Britain privatization has been quickly carried out without any notable opposition from the leading civil servants. In consequence, either the budget-maximization theory must be greatly exaggerated—there did not exist many inflated figures for the bureaucrats to defend—or else privatization was just a small adjustment like so many others over the years in a system that for the most part functions according to the same efficiency requirements as any other activity.[32]

One reason for not wanting to maximize the· budget is love of comfort. Attempts to do so incur not only political risks. Many bureaucrats also hesitate in the face of the uncertainty of the gains the considerable efforts required might yield as well as the increase in worries a larger staff always entails. One researcher expresses the dilemma of the utility-maximizing bureaucrat thus: 'should he strive for a larger budget which will increase his salary and his psychic income, or should he increase his ease of administration and his leisure through a smaller budget?'[33] Followers of the budget-maximization hypothesis, who are so critical of public administration of the present, seem to have forgotten the traditional critique of bureaucracy, not for being ambitious and energetic, but rather lethargic and without initiative.

A variant of the comfort argument is the fear the head bureaucrat might have of losing control. If an office grows quickly and a change occurs in its tasks and structure, this puts new pressures on a chief officer who wishes to maintain his leadership.[34]

Finally, it is just possible after all that the bureaucrats do not wish to spend time on budget maximization because they are 'mission-committed': they believe in their work and are loyally determined to put the intentions of the politicians into practice in an efficient manner.[35] Until such claims are systematically confirmed, however, they do not refute the budget-maximization hypothesis since they assume that which is to be proven.

A similar, by no means unreasonable but hardly conclusive, objection to the budget-maximization hypothesis is reported in a Swedish opinion poll. The bureaucrats themselves were opposed to an increase in allocations to national and local administration; like the citizenry as a whole, they wanted instead to reduce these expenditures—even more than other groups. However, it is possible that egoists amongst the bureaucrats wish to cut allocations for all agencies except their own.[36]

A more telling criticism of the budget-maximization hypothesis has been presented by a pair of American researchers who have studied the correlation between wage levels and the size of an administration. In essence, the idea behind their study is that bureaucrats want to maximize the budget because a larger budget is thought to lead to higher wages for the employees. We have already seen evidence that this relation does not always hold true. The authors' analysis of forty-five American bureaux on two occasions (March 1980 and

March 1985), with over 15,000 observations on each occasion, revealed that salaries were on the whole unaffected by an increase or decrease in the bureau's budget. The bureaucrats have employment benefits that protect them from such fluctuations.[37]

Thus when Niskanen's model has been confronted with studies from various countries and especially from the United States, his own point of departure, doubts have been raised concerning the accuracy of his hypothesis. It seems that bureaucrats neither may, can, dare, nor want to maximize the budget in the manner Niskanen assumed they would. In short, it has turned out to be very difficult to discover any scientific support for the budget-maximization hypothesis; it has been an easier matter to find objections and criticisms.

On the whole, in other words, political scientists answer 'no' to the question of the title of this chapter: bureaucrats are not budget-maximizers. A few quotations from summary assessments cast further light on the present state of research. 'In general, the empirical studies offer little support for the budget maximization hypothesis.'[38] 'The best known theory is Niskanen's (1971), probably because it is logically and mathematically elegant, although empirically false on each main point.'[39] 'There is not any empirical evidence to support the hypothesis . . . On the contrary. Whenever Niskanen's assumptions have been tested they have been falsified.'[40] 'Extensive theoretical as well as empirical' research demonstrates that the budget-maximization hypothesis 'does not hold as an explanation to the expansion of the public sector'.[41]

Sometimes the author's point is weakened by emotional arguments unusual in scientific presentations. 'To construct a theory of the growth of government on the self-interest of individuals is to turn politics into an asocial or antisocial activity', moralizes Richard Rose.[42] And Robert Goodin proclaims the whole notion of budget-maximization to be 'dead wrong' and calls for 'exorcism' to drive out the self-interest hypothesis from the theoretical constructs of rationalism.[43]

Nevertheless, researchers continue to refer to the budget-maximization hypothesis. This can be interpreted as an expression of the instrumental view of knowledge that was criticized in the introductory chapter, for the budget-maximization hypothesis is an excellent predictor of that which is to be explained. Whether it also provides a true picture of the actual mechanisms behind the expansion of the public sector is quite another matter, one which deeply worries an empiricist but hardly bothers an instrumentalist.

A couple of public-choice studies of Swedish agricultural policy show how it is possible by adopting an instrumentalist approach to give artificial respiration to a dead hypothesis. In a report from the Swedish University of Agricultural Sciences the author says that he wishes to put forward 'a new look at Swedish agricultural policy'. But almost the whole report is simply an account of various public-choice theories. Not until the last four pages does the author present some 'hypotheses concerning Swedish agricultural policy'. No attempt is made to test them, however.[44]

In a second study reference is made to Niskanen and other public-choice theoreticians in an analysis of the development of the agricultural sector in Sweden towards ever greater regulation, segmentation, and corporativism, something which has favoured the farmers' interests. However, public choice is not about something as general as the success of a minority in asserting its interests; that is common property of many theories in political science. What the school claims is that it is the self-interest of the actors that explains politics—in this case it would be the self-interest of the budget-maximizing agricultural bureaucracy. When reading this book one cannot repress the reflection that the very opposite may be true: that it is in the parliamentary competition that the farmers have been successful and that it is the actions of the agriculturally oriented parties (Lantmannapartiet, Bondeförbundet, and Centerpartiet) that have persuaded the Riksdag to incorporate the regulation of agricultural prices into Swedish welfare policy. Once again we meet a conclusion formulated as a hypothesis: 'The question is whether the policy of regulation corresponds most clearly to the interests of the bureaucracy in charge of administering the regulations—an alliance formed by the bureaucracies of state agencies, cooperatives, and private organizations together.'[45]

Instead of searching for evidence these scholars thus devote their time to suggestive persuasion. They cite their favourite hypothesis copiously and paint vivid descriptions of that which is to be explained, but they hardly broach the problem of the nature of the empirical relations that are presumed to connect the dependent and independent variables.

Adopting an instrumentalist approach instead of striving for realism in model construction characterizes many of those researchers who make use of economic models to explain political action. A further example is an article with the highly interesting title 'Voters, Bureaucrats and Legislators: A Rational-Choice Perspective on the Growth of Bureaucracy'. Although the authors here present a purely theoretical model, a certain view of reality is nevertheless suggested: given certain conditions, the bureaucracy expands without limit. Some particular factors facilitating this process are proposed, of which several appear rather strange—for example, the electoral system of majority voting adopted in Great Britain and France is considered to lead to a quicker growth of the bureaucracy there than in countries with a proportional system, such as the Scandinavian countries, the Netherlands, Belgium, Australia, and Israel. Whether or not this reflects reality is something the authors do not bother to look into.[46]

The most important step forward since Niskanen seems to be the so-called 'principal–agent model'. The idea is that politicians are not so naïve as to think that they are advised by disinterested experts and that they will take measures to reassert control over their subordinates. However, the agent knows something the principal does not, and there is a risk that the agent will exploit this edge strategically. What can the politician-principal do to induce the bureaucrat-agent to act in the principal's interest? In the Niskanen tradition a lot of formalized models have been discussed; fewer have been presented of a sort that seems fruitful for the study of existing bureaucracies and, unfortunately for the purposes of the present book, very few empirical results have been produced. To quote a review article: 'Currently it is fair to say that in political science principal–agent models are more talked about than written down.'[47]

But how can it be that the public sector has grown to be so large if the main cause is not the self-interest of the bureaucrats? Let us examine a few other explanations.

OTHER EXPLANATIONS

In a democracy the citizens get the state they ask for: that is, quite simply, the consumer perspective as an explanation of the size of the public sector. The public-choice school has complemented this with a producer perspective: the citizens get the public services that politicians and bureaucrats offer them. These two perspectives have been developed for the analysis of individual transactions in the economic market. Decisions concerning collective goods in the form of political operations of various sorts are not the result of the positions explicitly adopted by individuals but rather arise in the tension between economically unfettered demand and a general aversion to making a contribution to the cost. If one wishes to explain the growth of the public sector, one should therefore include a third perspective as well—the financial perspective.

In addition, it is usual in research on the public sector to distinguish between three different levels of explanation: a socio-economic, an ideological, and an institutional level.

In searching for explanations of the growth of the public sector other than that provided by the bureaucrats' self-interest, Daniel Tarschys, in a celebrated article, combines these three perspectives and three levels to yield nine different explanations that scholars have put forward to account for the expansion of the public sector. The following summary of these nine explanations is taken rather mechanically from Tarschys's own presentation.

A combination of the consumer perspective with the socio-economic level brings to mind changes in national income, industrialization, and urbanization. There is a tendency for the public sector to be larger at higher levels of economic development. This is called Wagner's Law, put forward a hundred years ago by the German economist and armchair socialist, Adolph Wagner. Before him, the opposite relation had been thought to hold true: as mankind developed morally and economically, the need for political authority would decline and gradually disappear altogether. People would no longer need any political leadership. This view was also shared by young socialists, including Karl Marx. Today endless examples confirm Wagner's Law. Increased geographical mobility, an increasing number of elderly people, more and more advanced technology—these make ever new claims on public services.

The ideological consumer perspective deals with changes in people's attitudes. Changes in communication and mass media increase the hopes and expectations the citizens hold with regard to the public sector.

The institutional consumer perspective states that changes in the political system itself can lead to increased demands on the public sector. One example might be a change in the electoral system by which the introduction of a proportional system is presumed to lead to increased demands on the bureaucracy. In grudging admiration of the ability of scholars to generate new hypotheses—which unfortunately is not balanced by a corresponding interest in testing them—we might note that this suggestion is the direct opposite of one above, that the 'first-past-the-post' system stimulates growth of the public sector.[48] Other explanations of this type might be the emergence of political parties and interest organizations that articulate new demands for public services.

The financial perspective in combination with all three levels deals with taxes. The socio-economic factors suggest that it is easier to tax an advanced society that has gone beyond a barter economy and large agricultural sector, a society in which care of children and the elderly has been taken over by the public sector, a large number of household chores have become commercialized, and women have entered the job market.

At the ideological level, certain researchers maintain that citizens are less unwilling to pay tax when their incomes rise, whereas others deny this. The legitimacy of the government is considered by most scholars to be important: it is easier to collect taxes in countries in which the government is well regarded and there is little corruption.

The financial–institutional factors comprise amongst other things the method of taxation itself: the number of bodies that can levy taxes (state, province, municipality, church) and the effect of the progressiveness of taxation with rising incomes are examples of this type of explanation.

Socio-economic changes are also considered to be of importance for the production of political activities. Particular mention is usually made in this connection of the efforts modern states make to counter unemployment. The rising costs of the public sector have been studied by social scientists ever since Wagner. Modern researchers point out that this phenomenon can be explained by the larger share of 'pure' services, for health care and education, for example, in the public sector as compared with the private.

Ideological changes in the producer perspective comprise the demands raised by those employed in public service. Professional ethics are one such cost-pushing norm. What a doctor does depends less on what the patient asks for and more on what other doctors consider to be correct. The way in which individual civil servants handle an item of business depends to a large extent on what they know about the way other civil servants deal with similar business in accordance with the principle of equal treatment.

When we come finally to the institutional factors in the producer perspective, we arrive at the public-choice school. The citizens get the public sector that the politicians (Downs) or the bureaucrats (Niskanen) conceive of and put on the market.[49]

Discarding or de-emphasizing the budget-maximization hypothesis does not leave one by any means empty-handed when one tries to account for the increase of the public sector in the United States and Western Europe.

CONCLUSIONS

To follow the debate concerning bureaucrats as budget-maximizers is to listen to a lively and intelligent, at times even brilliant, conversation in which insights and hypotheses cross swords while the will to test the notion systematically is less well developed. In this theoretically top-heavy debate, with each new model more elegant than the last, the hypothesis lives on as if it stated something about reality, as if it were confirmed through observation and not merely the expression of an obstinate postulate. The aura of legend has arisen around the budget-maximization hypothesis and we become mesmerized into believing in its vitality by being confronted with it everywhere. On the popular television programme 'Yes Minister', Sir Humphrey Appleby says, 'The Civil Service does not make profits or losses. Ergo, we measure success by the size of our staff and budget. By definition, a big department is more successful than a small one . . . this simple proposition is the basis of our whole system.'[50]

No matter how such quips may tickle our prejudices and strengthen our impressionistic experiences, a scientific description must be founded on more systematic work. In this respect one is in the first place struck by the manifoldness and complexity inherent in the causal explanations offered. To trace the growth of the public sector to a single cause such as the bureaucracy's selfish interest in maximum budgets is, as the survey of the debate has shown, clearly to over-simplify matters. A number of conditions of the most various nature seem to be at work. At the same time, the relations between these conditions are themselves complicated. Simply to run Tarschys's coarse classification through a regression analysis in the hope of determining the explanatory power of the separate factors would not be worth the effort, since the factors are themselves so different from each other. It would not be possible to put a reasonable interpretation on the coefficients.

Here, as in so many other situations in which political decisions constitute the dependent variable, a rationalistic approach can be of help in sorting out one's thoughts. David Cameron's study of the growth of the public sector in eighteen countries between 1960 and 1975 is an excellent example of this procedure. He is interested in five explanations: economic growth, method of taxation, 'politics' (particularly party competition and party representation in the government), constitutional conditions, and the country's dependence on the outside world. It is true that he is able to substantiate individual correlations. But he is not able to come up with any explanation to speak of until he develops a model of the way in which the various factors interact with each other. He finds that the underlying cause is a country's dependence on the outside world, which in turn leads to a high degree of industrialization. As a result of this there arise strong trade unions and left-wing-dominated governments which raise demands for expensive welfare measures. In addition, international competition tends to lead to a concentration of industry and the adoption of collective wage negotiations. Where trade unions are powerful, there automatically emerge demands for social commitments from the state as compensation for a moderate stand on wages, which in turn is a prerequisite for sustained success against international competition. In these different ways there develops the same pressure from both political actors and trade unions to expand the public sector. But the chain of causation is complicated. Economic and social conditions set the potentials and limitations but the final link must always be the will of the leading decision-makers.[51]

In the second place, the problems of operationalization are formidable. Instead of studying actual budget-maximization, the researchers discuss the will and ability of the bureaucrats to undertake such action. It is often suggested that one reason the budget-maximization hypothesis has not been tested is that it cannot be tested.[52] It is formulated in such a way that, as one scholar has put it, it is 'bound to be true'[53]—i.e. it does not fulfil our requirement of openness. The difficulty is thought to lie in a lack of knowledge both about the marginal costs and the marginal utility any change in a bureau's budget would involve. Without such information, the researchers are as little able as the political sponsors to decide whether or not an agency's budget is too large.

We know however where such information can, in principle, be found. Costs and utility are nothing but expressions of the values of the voters and politicians and these we know a fair bit about through survey studies, election results, and party programmes, as well as through speeches and voting in Parliament. It must be admitted, however, that to construct supply and demand curves on the basis of such information is obviously a very large step.

In the third place, the empirical evidence sometimes appears to be contradictory. The thesis argued in an article can be exemplified in an arbitrary fashion, and the reader's uncertainty only increases when example is set against counter-example.

Despite all this our methodological rules do spell out with reasonable strictness the way in which empirical studies are to be conducted. Those scholars who have wanted to provide a general picture of the relation between politicians and bureaucrats in Western politics have, however, chosen to go by a different route than that marked out by Niskanen. In broad studies based on representative samples, the line of approach adopted in the studies on the budgetary process referred to in the beginning of this chapter has been followed; the question of whether it is self-interest or public interest that ultimately guides the actions of bureaucrats has not been directly addressed, however. As we have seen, the concept of role is of central importance in this research. An attempt is being made to determine which roles the politicians and bureaucrats play and what changes are taking place. The classical role of executor that Max Weber talked about still has pride of place. But other roles play a part. Thus in one image the politician makes the decisions and the bureaucrat executes them. In a second they are both concerned with politics, but whereas the bureaucrat represents facts and knowledge, the politician serves interests and values. In a third, their roles flow even more closely together and it is the politician who stands for passion and ideology, the bureaucrat for reflection and pragmatism. In a fourth, the roles coalesce into a pure hybrid: the political expert who switches from political to administrative assignments. But no matter how these roles in the decision-making process shift from one country to another, no matter how the attitudes of bureaucrats vary towards political democracy or on the left-to-right scale of party politics, researchers repeat how important it is for the bureaucrats to have the confidence of the politicians. Always to play with an open hand seems to remain the surest road to the top posts in the administration.[54]

However, a certain amount of contradiction in the empirical evidence must not prevent us from seeing the woods for the trees. A pattern does exist, and it can be discerned. True, one can come across bureaucrats who out of self-interest try to maximize the budget for their agencies—just as any subtle image of reality always contains mixed motives of self-interest and public interest. But these do not appear to be any decisive cause of the expansion of the public sector. The budget–maximization hypothesis explains too little, it explains only what happens at the margin. Other circumstances appear to be more important. The extensive debate over the hypothesis has exposed so many shortcomings that one is left with serious doubts about whether it captures any essential feature of Western bureaucracy at all. The lasting impression left by this research is its failure to uncover any convincing evidence. To put it briefly, the budget-maximization hypothesis is not sustained by empirical research.

5

Individual and Collective Rationality

UNINTENDED CONSEQUENCES

Even if one can still find learned scholars who dispute questions of method and problems of interpretation, the great majority of empirical researchers are by now agreed, as we have seen, that the hypothesis concerning the predominant role of self-interest in Western politics cannot be upheld. It is true that voters are guided to a great extent by economic motives, but it is not so much private economic advantage as assessments of the government's ability to manage the economy of the country as a whole that underlie these decisions. Politicians always intend to win an election but only in a few exceptional cases have they been shown to manipulate the economy to that end. Bureaucrats are as pleased as anyone when their work is successful but those researchers who have attributed to them the ambition to maximize their budget rather than to be loyal and do a good job have had an extremely difficult time of it trying to find empirical support for their view.

How is one to account for the fact that public interest thus seems to be of greater importance than self-interest in politics? This is the question to be discussed in this concluding chapter.

As we have seen, the proponents of the public-choice school have not been slow in ridiculing political scientists who naïvely believe that politicians, in contrast to everyone else, work to achieve the common good instead of to maximize their self-interest.[1] Social critics take the postulates of the school for granted: 'of course, people in the public sector are as much motived by self-interest as people in the private sector';[2] citizens are beginning to realize 'that human beings are never so selfish as in politics'.[3]

In light of the research findings presented above, these unqualified statements certainly appear to be uncalled-for. But before we delve into the main problem of explaining the prevalence of public interest as a motive force, let us not yet leave the public-choice school but rather carry its hypothesis to its logical conclusion and ask what the consequences would be if self-interest were to be as prevalent in politics as the school presumes.

To avoid misunderstanding, it might be appropriate to recall that the public-choice school has never claimed that it is a *good* thing that self-interest predominates—but not that it is such a bad thing either. Such value judgements are left to others. The school has sought only to provide the most penetrating analysis possible of the political decision-making process; for this purpose the most realistic and natural view seemed to be that self-interest is the primary motivating force in politics as in most fields of conduct. In intimate relation with its sister theory in the rationalistic family (the social-choice theory) the public-choice school has subsequently gone to some length to set out the consequences of selfish action: it is a dark picture they paint. If actors act selfishly, the outcome is worse than what would in principle be possible, given a certain set of preferences. Selfishness brings unhappy results. In this sense self-interest is deplored even by the public-choice school, not as a value in itself but because it leads to what Robert Merton has, in a famous phrase, called 'unintended consequences'.[4]

To illustrate this relation let us return to the voting paradox and the 'Prisoners' dilemma', for that is precisely what this problem is all about. The voting paradox shows, it will be remembered, that there does not exist any decision rule which guarantees that individual preferences will be transferred into collective decisions in a way the majority would approve of. With the set of preferences reflected by the utility values in the 'Prisoners' dilemma' as shown in Figure 1, the logic of collective action leads inexorably to the sub-optimum solution

Actor 1

	0,0	−2,+2
Actor 2		
	+2,−2	−1,−1

in the lower right-hand square of the matrix. The actors move away from the upper left-hand square both in the hope of getting +2 instead of 0 and for fear of getting −2 should the action of the other prisoner move them downwards or to the right; the stable solution is thus −1 for both. When the actors simply follow their own self-interest without care for what is best for others, they collaborate in bringing about an outcome that is worse for everyone. It should be emphasized that the utility values refer to the actors' subjective evaluation of the different outcomes of the game; they say nothing about whether a particular outcome constitutes an objective expression of the common good. In other words, the corpus of rational theory has brought home a fundamental point: individual rationality is not always the same thing as collective rationality.[5]

'Prisoners' dilemma' is one of the main topics in rational choice literature and I have no intention here of going into the variety of solutions suggested to deal with this problem. I would just like to point to two ways out of the dilemma, both relevant to the problem of this book and both equally logical: to change the punishments levied or to abandon self-interest. The former solution could be called the prescription of the public-choice school and will be presented in this section. The alternative route will be discussed as we move from theory to practice and inquire into how public interest arises in politics.

The public-choice school emphasizes that since it is collective goods that lead to unintended consequences, one should restore them as far as possible to the market where all costs are made visible. The problem with politics is that, as a result of distorted prices, the citizens do not realize what the consequences of their demands actually are. On the other hand, if crime is kept in check with well-balanced punishments and if benefits are related to actual costs the way they are in the market, no one can intentionally or unintentionally deceive or damage another. Consistent to his individualistic philosophy of society, James Buchanan writes that the characteristic feature of the market is that all action is voluntary and reciprocal. Nothing happens unless the parties are agreed.

A situation is judged 'good' to the extent that it allows individuals to get what they want to get, whatsoever this might be, limited only by the principle of mutual agreement. Individual freedom becomes the overriding objective for social policy, not as an instrumental element in attaining economic or cultural bliss, and not as some metaphysically superior value, but much more simply as a necessary consequence of an individualist-democratic methodology.

Now of course, a certain amount of government is necessary, Buchanan concedes, and he also warns against anarchy. The problem is that it is so very difficult to find a balance between freedom and coercion, for when one gives the collectivity a hand, one has soon lost a whole arm. Collective decision-making processes seem to be unrelenting in bringing about unfortunate and unintended consequences. The citizens see no further than their own noses, the state begins to grow and becomes much more powerful than intended, with the unavoidable result that decisions become much worse than might have been possible.

Why would an individual agree to each one of a sequence of collective decisions, separately taken, only to find that the sequence generates an undesired ultimate outcome? Once the question is put in this way, numerous analogies from personal experience are suggested. Perhaps the one that is most pervasive is eating. In modern affluence, individual choice behavior in eating, on a meal-by-meal basis, often leads to obesity, a result that is judged to be undesirable. The individual arrives at this result, however, through a time sequence in which each and every eating decision seems privately rational. No overt gluttony need be involved, and no error need be present. At the moment of each specific choice of food consumption, the expected benefits exceed the expected costs.

A person who notices these tendencies in his own behaviour can put himself on a stricter diet. The same restrictiveness ought also to be found within an expanding government—to safeguard freedom, voluntarism, and society's capacity to make rational decisions without welfare losses.[6]

There is, however, little the individual can set against the state in our day. Instead of market agreements and freely made exchanges, we are confronted by a state set above individuals with ambitions to achieve a monopoly through coercive regulation. 'Even if she is motivated primarily by relative poverty, the call girl who sells services to one among many potential rich clients retains more freedom than the ordinary citizen who faces the monopoly bureaucrat.'[7]

In a large-scale work, William Riker, another of the more prominent political scientists amongst the rationalists, has summarized the normative implications of the insights that have been won through this approach. By being systematically kept from information about costs and long-term consequences, the citizens demand a larger state than they actually want. The voting paradox and 'prisoners' dilemma' give one warrant to be sceptical of decisions made by majority rule. The decision-making process is cyclical in nature and characterized by manipulation. 'Majorities are at best temporary artifacts.' It is therefore necessary to take collective decisions for what they are and not attribute to them some higher values such as an expression of the true will of the people reached after thorough deliberation. To protect the freedom of the individual one should introduce into the constitution powerful limitations on the government: e.g. a bicameral system, a division of power, local self-government, independent courts, limited mandate periods, and regular elections. The most important finding of rational political science is said to be that it has shown why there is always a reason to be suspicious of the process through which individual preferences are transformed into collective decisions. 'The social amalgamations of individual values are . . . often inadequate—indeed meaningless—interpretations of public opinion.'[8]

The successes of the public-choice school have led to a shift in attitude within the social sciences. Under the impress of Keynesian economics, social scientists devoted their attention to 'market failures' for a long time; in situations in which private enterprise failed, the state ought to go in and compensate, regulate, and stimulate. Nowadays they are increasingly aware of the fact that even governments can fail and there is talk of both 'Market Failure and Government Failure'.[9]

Here is a sample of how a representative argument might run. Let us suppose that there is a society with fifteen individuals whose income is distributed by general vote. One might perhaps believe that this would lead to everyone having the same wage. But since the author presupposes—as something obvious—that all citizens are motivated by self-interest, an even distribution of income is not the best solution for anyone. A majority of eight people can decide that they shall have more money than the remaining seven. Indeed, since their selfishness has no bounds, they have no reason to feel satisfied until they have got everything and the minority has been left without any income. It is only then that a stable solution has, from a technical point of view, been reached, something which certainly no one, if asked at the start, would have given as their spontaneous answer. Under these circumstances, however, it is unlikely that the minority will accept a decision-making rule that leads to such an unfavourable result. Production (and thereby income available for distribution) will be sabotaged and this will in turn cause the majority to try to preserve its advantage through coercion. The social machinery will thus be on the verge of breaking down.

For the public-choice school, the solution is, as mentioned above, to remove decisions regarding certain values such as income distribution from the political arena to the market where no one can force anyone else. If it rains manna from heaven, it might be preferable to divide up the earth and let each person gather in as much as he can from his plot than to vote on the total distribution.[10]

One can also find more extreme formulations which, like ideal models, bring into sharp focus the views of the public-choice school. How is it that the market succeeds but the political system fails to give people what they want? The answer we have heard many times before: because collective decision-making causes the citizens to disregard the long-term consequences of their decisions.

Utility-maximizing individuals find fewer incentives for responsible behavior in the polity than in the market. Indeed, collective choice, whether direct or representative, is unusually productive of both irresponsible conduct and irrational policies. Collective choice generates frustration, alienation, and impotence in individuals and extraordinary collective inefficiencies and inequities. To politicize life is to invite individuals to ignore the consequences of their choices.

Since all behaviour is selfish and nothing can be done to change that fact—'all behavior is self-interested . . . abolishing self-interest is fruitless'—even action on the market leads sometimes to costs for others. The difference is, however, that on the market the principle of voluntarism implies that any attempt to shuffle costs on to others meets with immediate reprisals, whereas collective decisions by which some people bind others through the coercive power of the state are often deliberately designed to injure others. 'Give me your vote, and I'll give you somebody else's money!' On the market the unseen hand has worked miracles. In politics it has the opposite effect when voluntary action is replaced by coercion. If individuals try to improve their lot and redistribute their wealth through collective action, the result will be less wealth for them to share. The realization that collective choice often brings about unfortunate and unintended consequences should result in a greater say for the market. 'While collective choice stands in the sharpest contrast to the market, marginal improvements are possible. But of all improvements the most effective is a steady diminution of the scope of government.'[11]

Set politically determined prices to be consistent with the market price so that the voters will have a clear idea of what the consequences will be for different alternatives! Deregulate! Privatize! Let the citizens try to realize their preferences freely on the open market instead of through an arbitrary bureaucracy! So might the recommendations of the public-choice school be summarized. Individual and collective rationality are opposed to each other and there is no necessity for everyone to suffer from being bound to others. Human beings are motivated by their self-interest and if they have access to the coercive instruments of the collectivity they will use them to appropriate wealth from their fellows and bring about a general loss of welfare. Only the market with its sensitive price system can react against such destructive behaviour; when the results of political decisions lead to unfortunate results for all, these are only discovered gradually. In other words, let market forces permeate the whole economy and individuals will have a better chance of reaching their goals.

THE SHADOW OF THE FUTURE

The 'prisoners' dilemma' has presented the social sciences with a challenge. If each individual does what is best for him, everyone will be worse off as a result. But regardless of what others do, is the individual always better off if he acts selfishly? Under such circumstances how is it at all possible to imagine that people might act to serve the common good?

In the past decade a great many suggestions have been put forward as to how a collectively rational choice might be made in the 'prisoners' dilemma'. Upon further reflection it becomes apparent that the method proposed by the public-choice school of reducing the effect of unintended consequences by minimizing collective decision-making is not a true solution, since the purely logical problem remains, even though its importance in quantitative terms is reduced. The second strategy for escaping from the dilemma—finding some way to overcome self-interest—entails by contrast that the premises of the problem are more strictly accepted and a search is made for an outcome that is better than the sub-optimum one to which the actors otherwise are inexorably driven by the dominant strategies of this game.

How does one overcome a selfish action? One solution[12] might be to transform the prisoners into altruists who truly wish each other well. Whether we would in that case really be dealing with altruistic action is a question that preoccupies the philosophers. It would then be in the interest of each that the preferences of the other be realized and both would still be egoists of a sort. On the other hand, however, the word 'self-interest' would not say very much despite its apparent precision; it would become so elastic as to be useless and one might wonder how, with such a definition of the concept, a person could ever be said to act against his own interests.[13]

The way to escape the 'prisoners' dilemma' is thus to try to convince the actors that it is morally right to co-operate. A person should not think of himself but of the good of others. As we have seen, the public-choice school looks on exhortations like this one as evidence supporting its view of conventional political science as naïve and idealistic. Against this background, it is therefore more interesting to consider other proposals for furthering the common good through politics.

One of the premises of this book has been that it is possible to distinguish self-interest from public interest. As we wrote in the first chapter, of course, this does not prevent there being cases in which these interests coincide in the long run. In Figure 2, therefore, the circles partially overlap each other. The shaded segment constitutes the common good, including 'my' good as well. In the 'prisoners' dilemma', all gain from co-operation. 'Egoism' and 'co-operation' appear as two distinct strategies to be chosen, each of which leads to quite different outcomes for the individual. If everyone chooses the selfish strategy, the solution for all is the sub-optimum one of -1. If they all choose to co-operate on the other hand, they receive the higher utility value of 0. In other words, the question is how rational egoists can be made to co-operate.

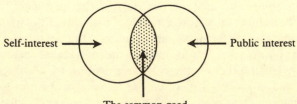

Self-interest   Public interest

The common good

Theories dealing with this question conceive of decisions made in 'the shadow of the future', to use a poetic expression. When the game of 'prisoners' dilemma' is repeated, there is a tendency for the actors sooner or later to end up in the upper left-hand square of the matrix. If the players are to meet again, they learn that it lies in their interest to co-operate to minimize losses. Even from a selfish point of view it is rational to try to bring about the second-best outcome and co-operate instead of being subjected to the second-worst outcome as a result of only thinking of oneself.

This general insight has been expressed more precisely in several renowned theories. One has been developed through a computer-based tournament concerning rational action in the 'prisoners' dilemma'. The winning strategy turned out to be 'tit-for-tat', according to which one begins by co-operating and thereafter acts in precisely the same fashion as the other player does on the move before. Another model, the 'assurance game', requires that one acts altruistically only on condition that the other player also does so, something which presupposes communication and confidence and a higher value on the utilities in the upper left-hand square. A third suggestion is the more contested theory of meta-games, which entails that the matrix is expanded such that one player makes his move bearing in mind the different alternatives that the other player can be imagined to choose; surprisingly, it turns out that the equilibrium solution in this case is different and more advantageous than that of the original matrix.[14] When the players meet on repeated occasions, the consequences of collective action are no longer unforeseeable. They learn to co-operate to avoid outcomes that are bad for both.

The problem at hand is a different one from that of developing a normative theory to achieve the common good. We already embrace the public interest, so to speak; the question is to explain how it has arisen.

If we juxtapose the empirical results of the three previous chapters with the argument just presented, showing how rational egoists find cause to co-operate on repeated runs of the 'prisoners' dilemma' game, the following picture emerges. In the world of politics, the consequences of different courses of action are not as unpredictable as they are in the market. The decision of the individual consumer has an infinitely small effect on the collective process by which prices are determined, a process it is of course impossible for him to observe immediately. The voter, on the other hand, makes a direct choice between a few already aggregated alternatives and the wishes of the various actors are known and publicly discussed. For this reason it is a simpler matter in the political game than it is in the market to estimate the likely outcome of various alternatives. If in the process the actors discover that they seem likely to bring about less acceptable outcomes, it remains possible for them to change strategy and produce more congenial decisions.

While the proponents of the self-interest hypothesis centre their hopes on setting satisfactory prices through market mechanisms, the representatives of the public-interest hypothesis believe in co-operation as a method to escape the 'prisoners' dilemma'. Both camps maintain that their particular world—the market and politics, respectively—is the more transparent, i.e. the one characterized by a minimum of unintended consequences. Although this may be true of the way the market functions ideally as a model, however, faulty information, limitations on competition, and other imperfections are quite evident in real-life economies. Politics, by contrast, because of its combination of collective organization and public debate, is probably easier to predict even in reality.

The self-interest hypothesis is not a good enough explanation when you go from economics to politics. In a well-received book, Howard Margolis maintains: 'For an empirically tenable theory of social choice, we require a model of individual choice which does not fail catastrophically in the presence of public goods. But the conventional model of choice does so fail, the most familiar illustration being the fact that it cannot even account for the elementary fact that people vote.' There are two Smiths residing within each individual, one oriented towards self-interest, the other towards public interest. The problem is to find an allocation rule to explain when either of these value systems prevails. Margolis suggests: 'The larger the share of my resources I have spent unselfishly, the more weight I give to my selfish interests in allocating a marginal bit of resources. On the other hand, the larger the benefit I can confer on the group compared to the benefit from spending a marginal bit of resources on myself, the more I will tend to act unselfishly.' When Smith makes his contribution to the Red Cross, he makes the usual assumption of diminishing marginal utility; similarly his contribution is marginal to the Red Cross. If Smith donates an additional $100 to the activity and simultaneously receives a $100 increment to his wealth, his public-interest orientation has changed but not his marginal utility from private spending. When a catastrophe occurs, this may cause a shift in Smith's perception of the marginal utility of his contributions. With such examples it should be possible to do systematic research on the development of the public-interest orientation in each individual. When economic models are applied outside the traditional market context, the egoistic model of man does not suffice.[15]

If everyone considers only his own self-interest in politics, the common good is thwarted—that seems to be, in all its simplicity, the very important insight that guides voters, politicians, and bureaucrats. The little extra I might get in my pocket-book if a certain party comes to power is less important than the loss in welfare everyone would suffer if, in my opinion, the party is in other respects unfit to govern or ideologically unacceptable. As important as it may be for a government to get re-elected, it generally hesitates to risk upsetting the stability of the economy by trying to create a political business cycle. The advantages a bureaucrat might possibly achieve if his own field of activity were to expand are nevertheless assessed by most administrators as less valuable than the damage they believe would be inflicted on the political system as a whole if the decisions of Parliament were not implemented as they were intended to be. In politics as opposed to the market (as these concepts have been ideally conceptualized here), it is both possible and judicious to find out how one's opponent is likely to act in different circumstances and to adapt one's own position accordingly in order to achieve the best possible outcome. Working out such strategies is something of the essence of politics. As a citizen, the task of the individual is not the same as that of a consumer with only his own utility to think of. The voters' choice, the politicians' decisions, and the bureaucrats' actions all imply judgements of what is best for society as a whole. The public interest is so much more widespread than the market-oriented proponents of the public-choice school would have believed likely.

Human beings are capable of thinking strategically. They can estimate how their fellows are likely to act under given circumstances, and they are able to strive for the second-best result when the position of the others makes it impossible to reach the best outcome. The public-choice school has a particularistic trait that gives it a tendency to disregard this possibility of rational co-operation; it releases only one group at a time from causal determinism and recognizes its ability to act independently. For Arrow the voters are central while the politicians and bureaucrats are like a sort of mechanical device for implementing the will of the voters (supposing that their will can be determined). In Downs, the politicians are dominant and gain control through vote-maximization over given structures of voters and bureaucrats. In Niskanen's model, it is the bureaucrats who are active in deceiving politicians and voters to accept far-reaching demands. By contrast, the picture that is painted in this book is truly rationalistic in that it assumes that voters, politicians, and bureaucrats are all influenced by each other and thereby understand how to act politically to bring about what they believe to be the common good.

FROM THE STATE OF NATURE TO THE WELFARE STATE

It is greatly to the credit of the public-choice school that it has brought our history of political thought to life. Behind the rationalists, philosophers, and electoral researchers who now discuss the place of self-interest and public interest in politics one can catch a glimpse of classical figures; even the terminology is often borrowed from earlier authors. It is not uncommon for example for proponents of the self-interest hypothesis to refer to Thomas Hobbes's description of the state of nature, in which egoism reigns unchecked and men are 'like wolves towards each other'. But instead of the absolutism of the Leviathan, the fire-breathing armoured crocodile from the Book of Job, for whose protection from this war of all against all mankind begs, a call is made for a new social contract to protect the freedom of the individual.[16] In doing so, the public-choice theorists come close to the ideas developed by such utilitarians as Jeremy Bentham and Adam Smith. The image of the rationally calculating, selfishly utility-maximizing individual largely coincides, as we have seen, with conceptions of 'economic man', whom the unseen hand leads to bring out, without intending to, that which is best for society as a whole.

Proponents of the public-interest hypothesis have found more inspiration from John Locke's sunnier picture of human life in the state of nature and, to an even greater extent, from Rousseau and his strong belief in the innate goodness of man. Rousseau's ingeniously elaborated version of the social contract has in particular inspired modern theoretical work. His analysis of how the individual submits his will to government because, as a citizen, he is himself a part of that government—how 'the will of all' is merged into 'the general will'—has been reconstructed as a description of how selfish actors learn to co-operate to escape the 'prisoners' dilemma' and achieve collectively rational solutions.[17]

In this way it lies in the interest of everyone that all choose a strategy of co-operation. In putting the matter in these terms we also hear a distant echo of Immanuel Kant's contribution to the debate, referred to in Chapter 1, regarding how the common good can only be reached if individual actors allow themselves to be guided by 'ethical preferences' or 'convictions' about what is best for society as a whole.[18]

Finally, in this general survey of political thought there is reason not to forget the Scottish sceptic and empiricist, David Hume, that sharp-witted eighteenth-century philosopher with moderately conservative leanings. Human beings are neither good nor evil, he maintained, neither markedly egoistic nor altruistic. In actual fact they are rather well-disposed, at least towards those nearest and dearest to them; which is not to deny that they can sometimes be seized by jealousy, by greed for power, or by a craving for vengeance. That is the reason why laws and regulations, 'conventions', are necessary for social life. But these conventions do not originate from some social contract by means of which human beings once left the state of nature; Hume's powerful criticism of natural right is part of his lasting contribution to the history of political thought. Nor are the conventions the result of the rational deliberations of individuals; Hume rejected energetically the view of the utilitarians that human action could be reduced to so simple a principle as utility-maximization. Each society creates its own laws by itself and people obey them quite simply out of habit and because they believe them reasonable. In general, governments cannot refer to some higher authority. Hume took it for granted that most governments have arisen through violence and usurpation. On the whole, however, the citizens accept their government to maintain social peace and keep their agreements and contracts to make social life possible. In summing up Hume's argument on this point, an English historian writes that two prerequisites must be fulfilled. 'First, each person must communicate his willingness to engage in mutual restraint to the others who will share in the convention. Second, there must be agreement on the set of rules that will be followed.' What motive, Hume wonders, makes me return an object I have borrowed, for example? Not self-interest— that would rather lead me to keep it. Nor is it sympathy for the owner, for others can have greater need of the thing than he. And it cannot be public interest, for the owner might be a 'miser or fanatic' while I myself or others use the object for more socially beneficial purposes. No, I return the object because there is a legal convention that says that I should act thus. This convention does not have the slightest thing to do with any 'natural rights'; it is simply a norm of action people have agreed to follow. Its value can only be understood if one sees the action as a part of a general practice in the society. Sometimes some single action taken in accordance with a convention can lead to an unfavourable outcome. But when one considers *the consequences for society as a whole*, it is of the utmost importance that the conventions be respected.[19]

Bearing these classical references in mind, let us attempt to summarize what modern research in political science has to contribute to this centuries-old discussion on the nature of man and the origin of the state, on altruism and utilitarian morality, on human evolution from the state of nature to the welfare state.

The philosophers of the seventeenth and eighteenth centuries probably did not regard the drawing up of a social contract as a particular historic event, nor do rationalists of the present day see the path from the 'prisoners' dilemma' to the common good as a sequence of temporally distinct steps. The underlying thought is not necessarily that man is first selfish and then begins to co-operate. The social contract and the 'prisoners' dilemma' are instead both to be regarded as ideal models intended to clarify the deliberations and decisions of rational individuals. The state of nature and the lower right-hand square of the matrix describe the unfortunate alternative that befalls men when they follow one particular strategy, the social contract and the upper left-hand square represent that alternative which increases the welfare of all as a result of a second strategy. Human beings need not necessarily have experienced the unfortunate consequences of selfishness in order to choose the altruistic alternative. In their imaginations they can divine the consequences of selfish action, which some scholars call unintended, and correct their choice accordingly.

As can be seen, this explanation is the direct opposite of that proffered by the public-choice school. In their view, there will always be people who want to travel free when others pay for it; free-riding in connection with collective action results in a smaller cake for all to share. That such things do occur in reality is indisputable. But according to the results of empirical research presented above, this is not the dominant trait in Western politics. On the contrary, it might be said, people seem to perceive the consequences of free-riding and (to a considerable extent) refrain from giving it a try. They take to heart the dangers the public-choice school warns of, and do not cheat as much with their taxes as they probably could without getting caught, because they understand that total welfare would thereby be reduced for all.[20]

It is thus hard to claim that people in Western democracies of the present find themselves engaged in a war of all against all. Equally unrealistic is the belief that the common good might be brought about by mechanically adding up everyone's self-interest. On the contrary, it seems as if people are led to act in their political roles by certain 'convictions' about what is best for society as a whole, by certain ideologies. But let us not on this account see everything through rose-coloured spectacles. It takes all kinds to make a world—both those who are moved by self-interest and those moved by public interest (as well as diverse variations in between: 'group interest', 'class interest', etc.). Rousseau's belief in the unbounded goodness of human beings is a hypothesis as unnecessary in explaining modern politics as Hobbes's self-interest hypothesis is a distortion. Nor do we need to imagine that some form of Kantian ethic of duty is generally adhered to in society in order to understand why the public interest is as widespread as it actually is. Faithful to the rationalistic premisses of this study, we can hold to the belief that man is a rational being who endeavours to realize his preferences. We can agree with Hume that there is nothing to say in favour of the view that man is especially selfish or especially unselfish; such speculations are not needed for our account. An understandable ambition to eradicate the reputation of being naïve idealists must not seduce political scientists into denying the findings of their own empirical research. For the most part men try to further the public interest in politics. But they do so because they think that in the long run such policies are also to their own benefit.

Notes

1. SELF-INTEREST AND PUBLIC INTEREST

1. D. C. Mueller, *Public Choice* (Cambridge: Cambridge UP, 1979), 1.
2. W. H. Riker and P. C. Ordeshook, *An Introduction to Positive Political Theory* (Englewood Cliffs, NJ: Prentice-Hall, 1973), 9–10 and 62–9.
3. A. Downs, *An Economic Theory of Democracy* (New York: Harper & Row, 1957), 27, 287, 295, 28, and 21 resp.
4. J. M. Buchanan and G. Tullock, *The Calculus of Consent: Logical Foundations of Constitutional Democracy* (Ann Arbor, Mich.: Univ. of Michigan Press, 1969, 1st publ. in 1962), 17, 19–20, 27, 267, 284–5, 294 and 297–8.
5. G. Tullock, *The Politics of Bureaucracy* (Washington, DC: Public Affairs Press, 1965).
6. A. Downs, *Inside Bureaucracy* (Boston: Little, Brown and Co., 1967).
7. W. A. Niskanen, *Bureaucracy and Representative Government* (Chicago and New York: Aldine-Atherton, 1971).
8. K. J. Arrow, *Social Choice and Individual Values* (New Haven, Conn., and London: Yale UP, 1963; 1st publ. in 1951).
9. This point is further developed in L. Lewin, 'Utilitarianism and Rational Choice', *European Journal of Political Research* (1988).
10. J. G. March and J. P. Olsen, 'The New Institutionalism: Organizational Factors in Political Life', *American Political Science Review* (1984), 734–49.
11. A. Sen, 'Behaviour and the Concept of Preference', *Choice, Welfare and Measurement* (Oxford: Basil Blackwell, 1982), 54–73.
12. A. Weale, *Political Theory and Social Policy* (London: Macmillan, 1983); F. E. Oppenheim, 'Self-Interest and Public Interest', *Political Concepts: A Reconstruction* (Oxford: Basil Blackwell, 1981), 127; J. Elster, *Ulysses and the Sirens: Studies in Rationality and Irrationality* (Cambridge: Cambridge UP, 1979), 39 and *passim*.

13. Sen, 'Behaviour and the Concept of Preference', p. 71.
14. B. Barry, *Political Argument* (London: Routledge & Kegan Paul, 1965), 207.
15. J. Elster, *Sour Grapes: Studies in the Subversion of Rationality* (Cambridge: Cambridge UP, 1983).
16. Oppenheim, 'Self-Interest and Public Interest', p. 127.
17. Barry, *Political Argument*, pp. 179–80; J. C. Harsanyi, 'Morality and the Theory of Rational Behaviour', in A. Sen and B. Williams (eds.), *Utilitarianism and Beyond* (Cambridge: Cambridge UP, 1982), 55; J. A. Mirrlees, 'The Economic Use of Utilitarianism', in Sen and Williams (eds.), *Utilitarianism and Beyond*, p. 64.
18. C. L. Ten, *Mill on Liberty* (Oxford: Clarendon Press, 1980).
19. R. Dworkin, *Taking Rights Seriously* (Cambridge, Mass.: Harvard UP, 1977), 235.
20. P. J. Hammond, 'Utilitarianism, Uncertainty and Information', in Sen and Williams (eds.), *Utilitarianism and Beyond*, pp. 85–102.
21. John C. Harsanyi, *Essays on Ethics, Social Behavior, and Scientific Explanation* (Dordrecht and Boston: Reidel, 1976), 13; Harsanyi, 'Morality', pp. 39–62. On the first page of the latter article Harsanyi mentions Kant as one of his sources of inspiration.
22. A. Sen, 'Rational Fools', in Sen (ed.), *Choice, Welfare and Measurement*, pp. 84–106.
23. W. Lippmann, *The Public Philosophy* (London: Hamish Hamilton, 1955), 44.
24. G. Schubert, 'Is There a Public Interest Theory?' in C. J. Friedrich (ed.), *Nomos V: The Public Interest* (New York: Atherton Press, 1962), 162–76.
25. For a more detailed treatment of the doctrinal history sketched here see L. Lewin, B. Jansson, and D. Sörbom, *The Swedish Electorate 1887–1968* (Stockholm: Almqvist & Wicksell, 1972), 11–24.
26. A. Siegfried, *Tableau politique de la France de l'Ouest sous la Troisième République* (Paris: Colin, 1913); H. Tingsten, *Political Behavior: Studies in Election Statistics* (London: P. S. King & Son, 1937); R. Herberle, *From Democracy to Nazism: A Regional Case Study on Political Parties in Germany* (Baton Rouge, La.: Louisiana State UP, 1945).
27. W. S. Robinson, 'Ecological Correlations and the Behavior of Individuals', *American Sociological Review* (1950), 351–7.
28. See in particular C. Merriam and H. F. Gosnell, *Non-Voting: Causes and Methods of Control* (Chicago: Univ. of Chicago Press, 1924).
29. P. F. Lazarsfeld, B. Berelson, and H. Gaudet, *The People's Choice: How the Voter Makes up His Mind in a Presidential Campaign* (New York: Columbia UP, 1944); B. Berelson, P. F. Lazarsfeld, and W. N. McPhee, *Voting: A Study of Opinion Formation in a Presidential Campaign* (Chicago and London: Univ. of Chicago Press, 1954); A. Campbell, G. Gurin, and

W. E. Miller, *The Voter Decides* (Evanston, Ill., and White Plains, NY: Row, Peterson & Co., 1954); A. Campbell *et al.*, *The American Voter* (New York: John Wiley & Sons, 1960).

30. P. E. Converse, 'Survey Research and the Decoding of Patterns in Ecological Data', in M. Dogan and S. Rokkan (eds.), *Quantitative Ecological Analysis in the Social Sciences* (Cambridge, Mass., and London: MIT Press, 1969), 459.

31. Berelson, Lazarsfeld, and McPhee, *Voting*, pp. 308–9.

32. L. Lewin, *Folket och eliterna: En studie i modern demokratisk teori* (Stockholm: Almqvist & Wicksell, 1970).

33. V. O. Key, jun., *The Responsible Electorate: Rationality in Presidential Voting 1936–1960* (Cambridge, Mass.: The Belknap Press of Harvard UP, 1966).

34. The model is most clearly presented in Campbell *et al.*, *The American Voter*.

35. O. Petersson, *Väljarna och världspolitiken* (Stockholm: Norstedts, 1982), 119.

36. Barry, *Political Argument*, p. 297.

37. Oppenheim, 'Self-Interest and Public Interest', p. 138. Oppenheim takes express issue with Schubert's statement, cited above, that the concept of public interest 'makes no operational sense'.

38. J. R. Pennock, 'The One and the Many: A Note on the Concept', in Friedrich (ed.), *Nomos V*, pp. 177–82.

39. See the analysis above of Downs, *Economic Theory*, and Buchanan and Tullock, *Calculus of Consent*.

40. Elster, *Forklaring*, pp. 141–6.

41. See n. 19.

42. See n. 13.

43. Downs, *Economic Theory*, p. 27. Downs here follows Milton Friedman, 'The Methodology of Positive Economics', *Essays in Positive Economics* (Chicago: Univ. of Chicago Press, 1953). Concerning the discussion that this article gave rise to see the articles in F. Hahn and M. Hollis (eds.), *Philosophy and Economic Theory* (Oxford: Oxford UP, 1979), which begins with a reprint of Friedman's article. See also E. Nagel, 'Assumptions in Economic Theory', in A. Ryan (ed.), *The Philosophy of Social Explanation* (Oxford: Oxford UP, 1973), 130–8.

44. K. R. Popper, *Conjectures and Refutations: The Growth of Scientific Knowledge* (London: Routledge & Kegan Paul, 1972; 1st publ. in 1963), 97–119.

2.   DOES THE VOTER FOLLOW HIS POCKET-BOOK?

1. J. D. Barnhart, 'Rainfall and the Populist Party in Nebraska', *American Political Science Review* (1925), 527–40.
2. S. A. Rice, *Quantitative Aspects of Politics* (New York: Alfred A. Knopf, 1928).
3. An excellent survey is made by K. R. Monroe, 'Econometric Analyses of Electoral Behavior: A Critical Review', *Political Behavior* (1979), 137–73.
4. V. O. Key, jun., *The Responsible Electorate: Rationality in Presidential Voting 1936–1960* (Cambridge, Mass.: The Belknap Press of Harvard UP, 1966), 35.
5. Monroe, 'Econometric Analyses', p. 142.
6. G. H. Kramer, 'Short-Term Fluctuations in U.S. Voting Behavior, 1896–1964', *American Political Science Review* (1971), 131–43.
7. G. J. Stigler, 'General Economic Conditions and National Elections', *American Economic Review* (1973), 160–71.
8. F. Arcelus and A. H. Meltzer, 'The Effect of Aggregate Economic Variables on Congressional Elections', *American Political Science Review* (1975), 1232–9.
9. S. Goodman and G. H. Kramer, 'Comment on Arcelus and Meltzer: The Effect of Aggregate Economic Conditions on Congressional Elections', *American Political Science Review* (1975), 1255–65.
10. H. S. Bloom and H. D. Price, 'Voter Response to Short-Run Economic Conditions: The Asymmetric Effect of Prosperity and Recession', *American Political Science Review* (1975), 1240–54.
11. F. Arcelus and A. H. Meltzer, 'Aggregate Economic Variables and Votes for Congress: A Rejoinder', *American Political Science Review* (1975), 1266–9.
12. E. R. Tufte, 'Determinants of the Outcomes of Midterm Congressional Elections', *American Political Science Review* (1975), 812–26.
13. E. R. Tufte, *Political Control of the Economy* (Princeton, NJ: Princeton UP, 1978); L. Sigelman and Yung-Mei Tsai, 'Personal Finances and Voting Behavior: A Reanalysis', *American Politics Quarterly* (1981), 371–99.
14. K. L. Schlozman and S. Verba, *Injury to Insult: Unemployment, Class, and Political Response* (Cambridge, Mass., and London: Harvard UP, 1979), 281–2.
15. G. H. Kramer, 'The Ecological Fallacy Revisited: Aggregate- versus Individual-Level Findings on Economics and Elections, and Sociotropic Voting', *American Political Science Review* (1983), 92–111.

16. S. Feldman, 'Economic Self-Interest and the Vote: Evidence and Meaning', *Political Behavior* (1984), 231.

17. C. H. Achen, 'Toward Theories of Data: The State of Political Methodology', in A. W. Finifter (ed.), *Political Science: The State of the Discipline* (Washington, DC: The American Political Science Association, 1983), 88.

18. M. P. Fiorina, 'Economic Retrospective Voting in American National Elections: A Micro-Analysis', *American Journal of Political Science* (1978), 426–43. Fiorina later published a larger study, *Retrospective Voting in American National Elections* (New Haven, Conn.: Yale UP, 1981), in which the theoretical approach was further developed. At a time when the writing of articles was on the increase in American political science, this work holds special interest inasmuch as it is a book on the large, old-fashioned scale of the electoral studies of the 1960s.

19. J. W. Wides, 'Perceived Economic Competency and the Ford/Carter Election', *Public Opinion Quarterly* (1979), 535–43; see also J. W. Wides, 'Self-Perceived Economic Change and Political Orientations: A Preliminary Exploration', *American Politics Quarterly* (1976), 395–411.

20. Schlozman and Verba, *Injury to Insult*, pp. 331–2.

21. M. S. Weatherford, 'Economic Conditions and Electoral Outcomes: Class Differences in the Political Response to Recession', *American Journal of Political Science* (1978), 917–38.

22. J. R. Hibbing and J. R. Alford, 'The Electoral Impact of Economic Conditions: Who is Held Responsible?' *American Journal of Political Science* (1981), 435–9.

23. J. R. Owens and E. C. Olson, 'Economic Fluctuations and Congressional Elections', *American Journal of Political Science* (1980), 469–93.

24. P. E. Meehl, 'The Selfish Voter Paradox and the Thrown-Away Vote Argument', *American Political Science Review* (1977), 11–30.

25. D. R. Kinder and D. R. Kiewiet, 'Economic Discontent and Political Behavior: The Role of Personal Grievances and Collective Economic Judgments in Congressional Voting', *American Journal of Political Science* (1979), 495–527.

26. D. R. Kinder and D. R. Kiewiet, 'Sociotropic Politics: The American Case', *British Journal of Political Science* (1981), 129–61.

27. D. R. Kiewiet, *Macroeconomics and Micropolitics: The Electoral Effects of Economic Issues* (Chicago and London: Univ. of Chicago Press, 1983), 130–1.

28. D. O. Sears, C. P. Hensler, and L. K. Speer, 'Whites' Opposition to "Busing": Self-Interest or Symbolic Politics?' *American Political Science Review* (1979), 369–84.

29. D. O. Sears *et al.*, 'Self-Interest vs. Symbolic Politics in Policy Attitudes and Presidential Voting', *American Political Science Review* (1980), 670–84.

30. D. O. Sears and R. R. Lau, 'Inducing Apparently Self-Interested Political Preferences', *American Journal of Political Science* (1983), 223–52.
31. M. S. Weatherford, 'Economic Voting and the "Symbolic Politics" Argument: A Reinterpretation and Synthesis', *American Political Science Review* (1983), 158–74.
32. Sigelman and Yung-Mei Tsai, 'Personal Finances'.
33. D. Rivers, 'Microeconomics and Macroeconomics: A Solution to the Kramer Problem', unpubl. paper, March 1986.
34. G. B. Markus, 'The Impact of Personal and National Economic Conditions on the Presidential Vote: A Pooled Cross-Sectional Analysis', unpubl. paper, March 1986.
35. S. Feldman, 'Economic Self-Interest and Political Behavior', *American Journal of Political Science* (1982), 446–66; Feldman, 'Economic Self-Interest and the Vote', p. 248.
36. A. I. Abramowitz, 'Economic Conditions, Presidential Popularity, and Voting Behavior in Midterm Congressional Elections', *Journal of Politics* (1985), 31–43.
37. P. Johnston Conover, S. Feldman, and K. Knight, 'Judging Inflation and Unemployment: The Origins of Retrospective Evaluations', *Journal of Politics* (1986), 565–88.
38. The European research in this field is considerably more difficult to summarize than the American. The following survey is based on traditional reviews of journals and literature, data searches in a few of the large American and European data bases, the assistance of colleagues from the official representatives of twenty or so member-institutes of the European Consortium for Political Research, and special information that has been kindly given me by the following scholars: Peter Aimer, University of Queensland; Ole Borre, Aarhus Universitet; Kevin Featherstone, University of Stirling; Giorgio Freddi, Università di Bologna; Christian Haerpfer, Institut für Konfliktforschung, Vienna; Barbara Haskel, McGill University; Michael Lewis-Beck, University of Iowa; Ola Listhaug, Universitet i Trondheim; Walter Santagata, Università degli Studi di Torino; Bo Särlvik, Göteborgs Universitet; Colette Ysmal, Fondation Nationale des Sciences Politiques.
39. Cited e.g. by D. A. Hibbs, 'On the Demand for Economic Outcomes: Macroeconomic Performance and Mass Political Support in the United States, Great Britain, and Germany', *Journal of Politics* (1982), 426.
40. M. S. Lewis-Beck, 'Comparative Economic Voting: Britain, France, Germany, Italy', *American Journal of Political Science* (1986), 315–46.
41. D. Butler and D. Stokes, *Political Change in Britain: The Evolution of Electoral Choice* (London and Basingstoke: Macmillan, 1974; 1st publ. in 1969), 378–402, and esp. at pp. 388–9 and 415.

42. J. Alt, *The Politics of Economic Decline: Economic Management and Political Behaviour in Britain Since 1964* (Cambridge: Cambridge UP, 1979), 187–99 and 223.

43. H. Rattinger, 'Collective and Individual Economic Judgments and Voting in West Germany, 1961–1984', *European Journal of Political Research* (1986), 393–419; D. Oberndörfer, H. Rattinger, and K. Schmitt (eds.) *Wirtschaftlicher Wandel, religiöser Wandel und Wertwandel: Folgen für das politische Verhalten in der Bundesrepublik Deutschland* (Ordo Politicus, 25; Berlin: Duncker & Humblot, 1985).

44. Kinder and Kiewiet, 'Economic Discontent', and 'Sociotropic Politics'; Feldman, 'Economic Self-Interest and Political Behavior'.

45. M. S. Lewis-Beck, 'Economic Conditions and Executive Popularity: The French Experience', *American Journal of Political Science* (1980), 306–23; M. S. Lewis-Beck, 'Economics and the French Voter: A Microanalysis', *Public Opinion Quarterly* (1983), 347–60, esp. p. 355; M. S. Lewis-Beck, 'Economics and Electoral Behavior in France', in N. J. Vig and S. E. Schier (eds.), *Political Economy in Western Democracies* (London: Holmes and Meier, 1985), 284–303. In his comparative article Lewis-Beck returns to the cultural difference between the USA and Western Europe but does so in connection with well-substantiated data that had been produced in response to quite a different question, namely whether voters consider that government policy has any effect at all in improving or worsening the economy of their personal household. In Great Britain 48 per cent thought it does, compared to 49 per cent in France, 43 per cent in West Germany, and 42 per cent in Italy. Lewis-Beck assured the reader that these figures were higher than those that could be obtained in the USA and referred to the studies by Feldman and others (Lewis-Beck, 'Comparative Economic Voting', p. 338). Feldman reports lower figures for the American voters but not dramatically lower: 35 per cent saw a connection between the administration's policy and their personal financial circumstances (Feldman, 'Economic Self-Interest and Political Behavior', p. 451).

46. T. D. Lancaster and M. S. Lewis-Beck, 'The Spanish Voter: Tradition, Economics, Ideology', *Journal of Politics* (1986), 648–74.

47. Paper from Christian Haerpfer's research project 'Value Change in Austria', Institut für Konfliktforschung, Vienna 1987.

48. G. A. Irwin, ' "It All Depends on How You Look at It": Changes in Thinking About Politics and the Vote in the Netherlands', paper presented at the Joint Sessions of Workshops of the European Consortium for Political Research, Gothenburg, 1986.

49. S. Holmberg, *Väljare i förändring* (Stockholm: Liber, 1984), 129–59.

50. S. Holmberg, *Svenska väljare* (Stockholm: Liber, 1981), 264–5.

51. S. Holmberg and M. Gilljam, *Väljare och val i Sverige* (Stockholm: Bonniers, 1987), 148–9.
52. A. Hadenius, *A Crisis of the Welfare State? Opinions about Taxes and Public Expenditure in Sweden* (Stockholm: Almqvist & Wicksell International, 1986), 121.
53. O. Listhaug and A. H. Miller, 'Public Support for Tax Evasion: Self-Interest or Symbolic Politics?' *European Journal of Political Research* (1985), 265–82.
54. A. H. Miller and O. Listhaug, 'Economic Effects on the Vote in Norway', *Political Behavior* (1984), 301–19. For a critique of their way of using prospective questions in interviews see however Holmberg, *Väljare i förandring*, p. 133.
55. B. O. Aardal and O. Listhaug, 'Economics and Voting Behavior in Norway 1965–1985', paper presented at the Joint Sessions of Workshops of the European Consortium for Political Research, Gothenburg, 1986.
56. O. Borre, 'Ideology and Class Voting in Denmark: A Preliminary Analysis', paper presented at the Joint Sessions of Workshops of the European Consortium for Political Research, Freiburg, 1983.
57. J. R. Happy, 'Personal Experience and Goverment Responsibility for Economic Performance in Canadian Voting Behaviour', paper presented at the Annual Meeting of The American Political Science Association, Washington, 1984.
58. K. Monroe and L. Erickson, 'The Economy and Political Support: The Canadian Case', *Journal of Politics* (1986), 616–47.
59. R. Johnston, *Public Opinion and Public Policy in Canada* (Toronto: Univ. of Toronto Press, 1986), 130–4, 123, and 144.
60. S. Reed and G. G. Brunk, 'A Test of Two Theories of Economically Motivated Voting: The Case of Japan', *Comparative Politics* (1984), 55–66. On the problem of cultural values and economic voting in Japan see also S. C. Flanagan, 'Value Cleavages, Economic Cleavages, and the Japanese Voter', *American Journal of Political Science* (1980), 195–6.
61. M. S. Lewis-Beck and H. Eulau, 'Introduction: Economic Conditions and Electoral Behavior in Transnational Perspective', in H. Eulau and M. S. Lewis-Beck (eds.), *Economic Conditions and Electoral Outcomes: The United States and Western Europe* (New York: Agathon Press, 1985), 4.
62. See n. 26.
63. See n. 57.

3. ARE POLITICIANS VOTE-MAXIMIZERS?

1. A. Downs, *An Economic Theory of Democracy* (New York: Harper & Row, 1957), 28, 96, 100, 112, and 279–94.
2. M. Kalecki, 'Political Aspects of Full Employment', *Political Quarterly* (1943), 322–31; G. Locksley, 'The Political Business Cycles: Alternative Interpretations', in P. Whiteley (ed.), *Models of Political Economy* (London and Beverly Hills: Sage, 1980), 177–98.
3. W. D. Nordhaus, 'The Political Business Cycle', *Review of Economic Studies* (1975), 169–90.
4. C. D. MacRae, 'A Political Model of the Business Cycle', *Journal of Political Economy* (1977), 239–63.
5. B. S. Frey, 'Politico-Economic Models and Cycles', *Journal of Public Economics* (1978), 203–20; B. S. Frey, 'Politometrics of Government Behavior in a Democracy', *Scandinavian Journal of Economics* (1979), 308–22, esp. pp. 316–22.
6. B. S. Frey and F. Schneider, 'Politico-Economic Models in Competition with Alternative Models: Which Predict Better?' *European Journal of Political Science* (1982), 241–54, esp. pp. 252–3.
7. E. R. Tufte, *Political Control of the Economy* (Princeton, NJ: Princeton UP, 1978), esp. pp. 11–12, 17–18, 26, and 105. For the critique of Tufte see e.g. M. Paldam, 'An Essay on the Rationality of Economic Policy: The Test-Case of the Electional Cycle', *Public Choice* (1981), 287–305, esp. p. 297, and the review of Jeff Fishel in *American Political Science Review* (1979), 1162–5.
8. B. T. McCallum, 'The Political Business Cycle: An Empirical Test', *Southern Economic Journal* (1977), 504–15.
9. M. Paldam, 'Is There an Electional Cycle? A Comparative Study of National Accounts', *Scandinavian Journal of Economics* (1979), 323–42.
10. Paldam, 'Essay on Rationality'.
11. J. Alt, 'Political Business Cycles in Britain', in Whiteley (ed.), *Models of Political Economy*, pp. 155–75.
12. J. Alt and A. Chrystal, 'Modelling the Growth of Government Expenditure in Advanced Industrial Societies', paper presented at the Annual Meeting of the American Political Science Association, New York, 1978.
13. R. Dinkel, 'Political Business Cycles in Germany and the United States: Some Theoretical and Empirical Considerations', in D. A. Hibbs, jun., H. Fassbinder, and R. D. Rivers (eds.), *Contemporary Political Economy: Studies on the Interdependence of Politics and Economics* (Amsterdam: North-Holland Publishing Company, 1981), 209–30.
14. D. Wittman, 'Candidate Motivation: A Synthesis of Alternative Theories',

American Political Science Review (1983), 142–57. See also D. Wittman, 'Parties as Utility Maximizers', *American Political Science Review* (1973), 490–8.

15. S. D. Allen, J. M. Sulock, and W. A. Sabo, 'The Political Business Cycle: How Significant?' *Public Finance Quarterly* (1986), 107–12.
16. U. Laurin, *På heder och samvete: Skattefuskets orsaker och utbredning* (Stockholm: Norstedts, 1986), 170, n. 31.
17. P. Whiteley, *Political Control of the Macroeconomy: The Political Economy of Public Policy Making* (London: Sage, 1986), 61–83.
18. H. W. Chappell, jun., and W. R. Keech, 'A New View of Political Accountability for Economic Performance', *American Political Science Review* (1985), 10–27.
19. U. Lächler, 'The Political Business Cycle under Rational Voting Behavior', *Public Choice* (1984), 411–30.
20. P. Minford and D. Peel, 'The Political Theory of the Business Cycle', *European Economic Review* (1982), 253–70.
21. R. Johnston, *Public Opinion and Public Policy in Canada* (Toronto: Univ. of Toronto Press, 1986), 120–4 and 144.
22. H. J. Madsen, 'Electoral Outcomes and Macro-Economic Policies: The Scandinavian Cases', in Whiteley (ed.), *Models of Political Economy*, pp. 15–46.
23. J. A. Lybeck, 'Finns det en politisk konjunkturcykel i Sverige?' *Ekonomisk debatt* (1983), 313–22; 'A Simultaneous Model of Politico-Economic Interaction in Sweden, 1970–82', *European Journal of Political Research* (1985), 135–51; and *The Growth of Government in Developed Countries* (Aldershot: Gower, 1986).
24. L. Jonung, 'Business Cycles and Political Changes in Sweden', *Skandinaviska Enskilda Banken Quarterly Review* (1985), 26–39.
25. A. Przeworski and J. Sprague, *Paper Stones: A History of Electoral Socialism* (Chicago and London: Univ. of Chicago Press, 1986). I thank Dr Jörgen Hermansson who directed my attention to this work.

4. ARE BUREAUCRATS BUDGET-MAXIMIZERS?

1. W. A. Niskanen, *Bureaucracy and Representative Government* (Chicago and New York: Aldine-Atherton, 1971), 39. In an article a few years later ('Bureaucrats and Politicians', *Journal of Law and Economics* (1975), 617–43), in which the author comments upon the debate in his book provoked, he modifies his description of the motives of bureaucrats to

include 'slack resources', a change which does not however affect his thesis in any vital respect. For valuable suggestions concerning literature for this chapter I am especially grateful to Dr Bo Rothstein (nn. 8, 25, and 40), Prof. Benny Hjern (n. 37) and Prof. Lars Strömberg (nn. 17 and 19).

2. A. Wildavsky, *The Politics of the Budgetary Process* (Boston: Little, Brown & Co., 1964); T. J. Anton, *The Politics of State Expenditure in Illinois* (Urbana, Ill.: Univ. of Illinois Press, 1966); H. Heclo and A. Wildavsky, *The Private Government of Public Money* (London: Macmillan, 1974); T. J. Anton, 'Roles and Symbols in the Determination of State Expenditures', in I. Sharkansky (ed.), *Policy Analysis in Political Science* (Chicago: Markham, 1970), 209–24.

3. R. E. Goodin, 'Rational Politicians and Rational Bureaucrats in Washington and Whitehall', *Public Administration* (1982), 23–41.

4. A. Breton, *The Economic Theory of Representative Government* (London and Basingstoke: Macmillan, 1974).

5. A. Breton and R. Wintrobe, 'The Equilibrium Size of a Budget-Maximizing Bureau: A Note on Niskanen's Theory of Bureaucracy', *Journal of Political Economy* (1975), 195–207.

6. G. J. Miller and T. M. Moe, 'Bureaucrats, Legislators, and the Size of Government', *American Political Science Review* (1983), 297–322.

7. B. L. Benson, 'Why are Congressional Committees Dominated by "High-Demand" Legislators? A Comment on Niskanen's View of Bureaucrats and Politicians', *Southern Economic Journal* (1981), 68–77.

8. G. A. Boyne, 'Bureaucratic Power and Public Policies: A Test of the Rational Staff Maximization Hypothesis', *Political Studies* (1987), 79–104.

9. R. Rose, *Understanding Big Government: The Programme Approach* (London: Sage, 1984), 45.

10. P. Self, *Political Theories of Modern Government* (London: George Allen & Unwin, 1985), 67–8.

11. J.-E. Lane (ed.), *Bureaucracy and Public Choice* (London: Sage, 1987). In this work see esp. R. J. Sørensen, 'Bureaucratic Decision-Making and the Growth of Public Expenditure', and A. Dunsire, 'Testing Theories: The Contribution of Bureaumetrics'.

12. R. M. Spann, 'Public Versus Private Provision of Governmental Services', in Borcherding (ed.), *Budgets and Bureaucrats*, pp. 71–89.

13. R. J. Staaf, 'The Growth of the Educational Bureaucracy: Do Teachers Make a Difference?', in Borcherding (ed.), *Budgets and Bureaucracy*, pp. 148–68.

14. W. Orzechowski, 'Economic Models of Bureaucracy: Survey, Extensions, and Evidence', in Borcherding (ed.), *Budgets and Bureaucracy*, pp. 229–59.

15. W. C. Bush and R. J. Mackay, 'Private Versus Public Sector Growth: A

Collective Choice Approach', in Borcherding (ed.), *Budgets and Bureaucracy*, pp. 188–210.

16. T. E. Borcherding, W. C. Bush, and R. M. Spann, 'The Effects on Public Spending of the Divisibility of Public Outputs in Consumption, Bureaucratic Power, and the Size of the Tax-Sharing Group', in Borcherding (ed.), *Budgets and Bureaucracy*, pp. 211–28.

17. P. M. Jackson, *The Political Economy of Bureaucracy* (Oxford: Philip Allan, 1982), 121–41.

18. J. C. Thoenig and E. Friedberg, 'The Power of the Field Staff: The Case of the Ministry of Public Works, Urban Affairs and Housing in France', in A. F. Leemans (ed.), *The Management of Change in Government* (The Hague: Martinus Nijhoff, 1976), 314–37.

19. E. Ostrom, 'Multiorganizational Arrangements and Coordination: An Application of Institutional Analysis' in F. X. Kaufmann *et al.* (eds.), *Guidance, Control, and Evaluation in the Public Sector* (Berlin and New York: de Gruyter, 1985), 495–510.

20. Self, *Political Theories*, p. 67.

21. G. P. de Bruin, 'Economic Theory of Bureaucracy and Public Good Allocation', in Lane (ed.), *Bureaucracy*, p. 58.

22. J. A. C. Conybeare, 'Bureaucracy, Monopoly, and Competition: A Critical Analysis of the Budget-Maximizing Model of Bureaucracy', *American Journal of Political Science* (1984), 479–502.

23. R. E. Goodin, 'Possessive Individualism Again', *Political Studies* (1976), 494.

24. Goodin, 'Possessive Individualism', p. 26.

25. P. Dunleavy, 'Bureaucrats, Budgets and the Growth of the State: Reconstructing an Instrumental Model', *British Journal of Political Science* (1985), 299–328.

26. J. Margolis, 'Comment', *Journal of Law and Economics* (1975), 646.

27. Breton and Wintrobe, 'Equilibrium Size', p. 205.

28. Goodin, 'Rational Politicians', p. 31.

29. Self, *Political Theories*, pp. 67–8.

30. Margolis, 'Comment', p. 648.

31. Breton and Wintrobe, 'Equilibrium Size', p. 204.

32. P. Dunleavy, 'Explaining the Privatization Boom: Public Choice Versus Radical Approaches', *Public Administration* (1986), 13–34.

33. Jackson, *Political Economy*, p. 133.

34. Breton and Wintrobe, 'Equilibrium Size', p. 198; Margolis, 'Comment', p. 658.

35. Margolis, 'Comment'; Goodin, 'Rational Politicians'; O. P. Kristensen, 'The Logic of Political-Bureaucratic Decision-Making as a Cause of Governmental Growth', *European Journal of Political Research* (1980), 255; K. J. Meier, *Regulation: Politics, Bureaucracy, and Economics* (New

York: St Martin's Press, 1985), 14. For a discussion of control and bureaucratic responsibility, see M. V. Nadel and F. E. Rourke, 'Bureaucracies', in F. I. Greenstein and N. W. Polsby (eds.), *Governmental Institutions and Processes: Handbook of Political Science*, v (Reading: Addison-Wesley, 1975), 415–29.

36. A. Hadenius, *A Crisis of the Welfare State? Opinions About Taxes and Public Expenditure in Sweden* (Stockholm: Almqvist & Wicksell International, 1986), 103–4.

37. R. N. Johnson and G. D. Libecap, 'Agency Growth and Bureaucratic Salaries', unpubl. paper, Montana State Univ. and Univ. of Arizona, June 1987.

38. Conybeare, 'Bureaucracy', p. 486.

39. Self, *Political Theories*, p. 67.

40. L. Ingemarson, 'Public Choice och den offentliga sektorns tillväxt i den industrialiserade västvärlden', unpubl. paper, Dept. of Economics, Univ. of Lund, 1986, p. 30. This analysis of different explanations to the expansion of the public sector follows Tarschy's well-known classification (see n. 49). The author begins by posing the following rhetorical question: 'Budget allocations to the defence and social departments in Sweden have developed in such a way between 1920 and 1980 that, apart from the exceptional conditions pertaining during the Second World War, the relative size of these budget items has been dramatically switched. Is the sole cause of this the fact that the civil servants in the defence department have been so much inferior to their counterparts in the social department when it comes to budget maximization?'

41. B. Rothstein, 'Litteraturgranskningar', *Statsvetenskaplig tidskrift* (1988), 243.

42. Rose, *Understanding Big Government*, pp. 44–5.

43. Goodin, 'Possessive Individualism', pp. 497 and 501. Despite his agitation Goodin thus managed to observe a distinction that many others neglect between the assumption that human beings are egoists and rationalistic theory as a form of open-ended, scientific explanation.

44. J. von Ehrenheim, *Public Choice: En ny syn på svensk jordbrukspolitik* (Uppsala: Swedish Univ. of Agricultural Sciences, 1984).

45. O. Bolin, P.-M. Meyerson, and I. Ståhl, *Makten över maten: Livsmedelssektorns politiska ekonomi* (Stockholm: SNS, 1984), 85.

46. M. P. Fiorina and R. N. Noll, 'Voters, Bureaucrats and Legislators: A Rational Choice Perspective on the Growth of Bureaucracy', *Journal of Public Economics* (1978), 239–54.

47. J. Bendor, 'Review Article: Formal Models of Bureaucracy', *British Journal of Political Science* (1988), 353–95; a rich collection of articles is to be found in C. K. Rowley, R. D. Tollison, and G. Tullock (eds.), *The Political Economy of Rent-Seeking* (Boston: Kluwer Academic Publ., 1988).

48. Fiorina and Noll, 'Voters'.
49. D. Tarschys, 'The Growth of Public Expenditures: Nine Modes of Explanation', *Scandinavian Political Studies* (1975), 9–31.
50. Quoted by Dunsire in Lane (ed.), *Bureaucracy*, p. 112.
51. D. R. Cameron, 'The Expansion of the Public Economy: A Comparative Analysis', *American Political Science Review* (1978), 1243–61.
52. Lane, *Bureaucracy*, p. 15; Fiorina and Noll, 'Voters', p. 251; B. Hjern, 'Vad optimerar byråchefen?' *Statsvetenskaplig tidskrift* (1973), 184; R. Greenwood, 'Bureaucracy: Servant or Master?' *Public Administration* (1974), 356.
53. Dunsire in Lane, *Bureaucracy*, p. 121.
54. J. D. Aberbach, R. D. Putnam, and B. A. Rockman, *Bureaucrats and Politicians in Western Democracies* (Cambridge, Mass., and London: Harvard UP, 1981); a Swedish study in connection with this comparative study is A. Mellbourn, *Byråkratins ansikten: Rolluppfattningar hos svenska högre statstjänstemän* (Stockholm: Liber, 1979); R. D. Putnam, 'The Political Attitudes of Senior Civil Servants in Western Europe: A Preliminary Report', *British Journal of Political Science* (1973), 257–90; M. Dogan (ed.), *The Mandarins of Western Europe: The Political Role of Top Civil Servants* (New York: John Wiley & Sons, 1975).

5. INDIVIDUAL AND COLLECTIVE RATIONALITY

1. See ref. to Downs above, Ch. 1 n. 3.
2. See e.g. K. Samuelsson, 'Den spräckliga högern', *Svenska Dagbladet*, 9 Nov. 1986; G. Heckscher, 'Konservatismen och utopierna', *Svenska Dagbladet*, 2 Nov. 1986.
3. O. Ehrencrona, 'Politik, egoism och altruism', *Svenska Dagbladet*, 12 Oct. 1986.
4. R. K. Merton, *Social Theory and Social Structure*, rev. edn. (New York: Free Press, 1957), 50–64.
5. A. Rapoport and A. M. Chammah, *Prisoner's Dilemma* (Ann Arbor: Univ. of Michigan Press, 1965); A. Rapoport, 'Prisoner's Dilemma: Recollections and Observations', in B. Barry and R. Hardin (eds.), *Rational Man and Irrational Society? An Introduction and Sourcebook* (Beverly Hills: Sage, 1982), 72–83.
6. J. M. Buchanan, *The Limits of Liberty: Between Anarchy and Leviathan* (Chicago and London: Univ. of Chicago Press, 1975), 2 and 149–50.
7. J. M. Buchanan, 'Political Equality and Private Property: The Distributional Paradox', in G. Dworkin, G. Bermant, and P. G. Brown (eds.),

Markets and Morals (Washington, DC, and London: Hemisphere Publishing Corporation, 1977), 82.

8. W. H. Riker, *Liberalism Against Populism: A Confrontation Between the Theory of Democracy and the Theory of Social Choice* (San Francisco: W. H. Freeman and Co., 1982), 234 and 238.

9. This was the title Buchanan gave his Nobel Lecture at Uppsala, 12 Dec. 1986. Compare C. Wolf, jun., 'A Theory of Nonmarket Failure: Framework for Implementation Analysis', *Journal of Law and Economics* (1979), 107–39.

10. D. Usher, *The Economic Prerequisite to Democracy* (Oxford: Basil Blackwell, 1981), esp. chs. 2, 5, and 6.

11. W. C. Mitchell, 'Efficiency, Responsibility, and Democratic Politics', in J. R. Pennock and J. W. Chapman (eds.), *Nomos XXV: Liberal Democracy* (New York and London: New York UP, 1983), 343–73.

12. Classifications of different possible ways of arriving at the common good in the 'prisoners' dilemma' can be found e.g. in J. Elster, *Forklaring og dialektikk: Noen grunnbegreper i vitenskapsteorien* (Oslo: Pax, 1979), 83–6, and D. Parfit, *Reasons and Persons* (Oxford: Clarendon Press, 1984), 63–6.

13. R. A. Dahl lets his perspicacity run through these conceptual labyrinths in *Polyarchy: Participation and Opposition* (New Haven, Conn., and London: Yale UP, 1971), 163–6.

14. Rapoport and Chammah, *Prisoner's Dilemma*; R. Hardin, *Collective Action* (Baltimore and London: The Johns Hopkins UP, 1982); D. Gauthier, 'Reason and Maximization', in Barry and Hardin (eds.), *Rational Man*; A. Sen, 'Rational Fools', in Sen (ed.), *Choice, Welfare and Measurement* (Oxford: Basil Blackwell, 1982); K. A. Oye, 'Explaining Cooperation Under Anarchy: Hypotheses and Strategies', *World Politics* (1985), 1–24; R. Axelrod and R. O. Keohane, 'Achieving Cooperation Under Anarchy: Strategies and Institutions', *World Politics* (1985), 226–54; J. Elster, 'Rationality, Morality, and Collective Action', *Ethics* (1985), 136–55; J. Elster (ed.), *Rational Choice* (Oxford: Basil Blackwell, 1986); W. H. Wilcox, 'Egoists, Consequentialists, and Their Friends', *Philosophy and Public Affairs* (1987), 73–84. For their valuable comments I wish to express special thanks to Associate Professors Barry Holmström and Olof Petersson as well as to Dr Jörgen Hermansson. On the computerized tournament, see R. Axelrod, *The Evolution of Cooperation* (New York: Basic Books, 1984); on the assurance game, see A. Sen, 'Isolation, Assurance and the Social Rate of Discount', *Quarterly Journal of Economics* (1967), 112–24, Elster, *Forklaring og dialektikk*, pp. 76–8 and 84–6, and J. Elster, *Ulysses and the Sirens: Studies in Rationality and Irrationality* (Cambridge: Cambridge UP, 1979), 18–28 and 141–4; on the meta-game, see N. Howard, *Paradoxes of Rationality: Theory of Metagames and Political Behavior* (Cambridge, Mass.: MIT Press, 1971).

15. H. Margolis, 'A New Model of Rational Choice', *Ethics* (1981), 265–79, and *Selfishness, Altruism, and Rationality* (Cambridge: Cambridge UP, 1982).
16. e.g. Buchanan's *The Limits of Liberty* carries the sub-title 'Between Anarchy and Leviathan' and several chapters deal with the concept of the social contract.
17. Jörgen Hermansson, 'Rousseaus teori om allmänviljan', unpubl. paper, Dept. of Government, Univ. of Uppsala, 1987.
18. In Ch. 1 n. 20 above Harsanyi refers specifically to Immanuel Kant.
19. D. Miller, *Philosophy and Ideology in Hume's Political Thought* (Oxford: Clarendon Press, 1981), 61–4.
20. U. Laurin, *På heder och samvete: Skattefuskets orsaker och utbredning* (Stockholm: Norstedts, 1986).

Bibliography

AARDAL, BERNT OLAV, and LISTHAUG, OLA, 'Economics and Voting Behavior in Norway 1965–1985', paper presented at the Joint Sessions of Workshops of the European Consortium for Political Research, Gothenburg, 1986.

ABERBACH, JOEL D., PUTNAM, ROBERT D., and ROCKMAN, BERT A., *Bureaucrats and Politicians in Western Democracies* (Cambridge, Mass., and London: Harvard UP, 1981).

ABRAMOWITZ, ALAN I., 'Economic Conditions, Presidential Popularity, and Voting Behavior in Midterm Congressional Elections', *Journal of Politics* (1985).

ACHEN, CHRISTOPHER H., 'Toward Theories of Data: The State of Political Methodology', in Ada W. Finifter (ed.), *Political Science: The State of the Discipline* (Washington, DC: The American Political Science Association, 1983).

ALLEN, STUART D., SULOCK, JOSEPH M., and SABO, WILLIAM A., 'The Political Business Cycle: How Significant?' *Public Finance Quarterly* (1986).

ALT, JAMES, *The Politics of Economic Decline: Economic Management and Political Behaviour in Britain Since 1964* (Cambridge etc.: Cambridge UP, 1979).

—— 'Political Business Cycles in Britain', in Whiteley (ed.), *Models of Political Economy*.

—— and CHRYSTAL, ALEC, 'Modelling the Growth of Government Expenditure in Advanced Industrial Societies', paper presented at the Annual Meeting of The American Political Science Association, New York, 1978.

ANTON, THOMAS J., *The Politics of State Expenditure in Illinois* (Urbana, Ill.: Univ. of Illinois Press, 1966).

—— 'Roles and Symbols in the Determination of State Expenditures', in Ira Sharkansky (ed.), *Policy Analysis in Political Science* (Chicago: Markham, 1970).

ARCELUS, FRANCISCO, and MELTZER, ALLAN H., 'The Effect of Aggregate Economic Variables on Congressional Elections', *American Political Science Review* (1975).

—— 'Aggregate Economic Variables and Votes for Congress: A Rejoinder', *American Political Science Review* (1975).

ARROW, KENNETH J., *Social Choice and Individual Values* (New Haven, Conn., and London: Yale UP, 1963; 1st publ. in 1951).

AXELROD, ROBERT, *The Evolution of Cooperation* (New York: Basic Books, 1984).

—— and KEOHANE, ROBERT O., 'Achieving Cooperation Under Anarchy: Strategies and Institutions', *World Politics* (1985).

BARNHART, JOHN D., 'Rainfall and the Populist Party in Nebraska', *American Political Science Review* (1925).

BARRY, BRIAN, *Political Argument* (London: Routledge & Kegan Paul, 1965).

—— and HARDIN, RUSSELL (eds.), *Rational Man and Irrational Society? An Introduction and Sourcebook* (Beverly Hills and London: Sage, 1982).

BENDOR, JONATHAN, 'Review Article: Formal Models of Bureaucracy', *British Journal of Political Science* (1988).

BENSON, BRUCE L., 'Why Are Congressional Committees Dominated by "High-Demand" Legislators? A Comment of Niskanen's View of Bureaucrats and Politicians', *Southern Economic Journal* (1981).

BERELSON, BERNARD, LAZARSFELD, PAUL F., and McPHEE, WILLIAM N., *Voting: A Study of Opinion Formation in a Presidential Campaign* (Chicago and London: Univ. of Chicago Press, 1954).

BLOOM, HOWARD S., and PRICE, H. DOUGLAS, 'Voter Response to Short-Run Economic Conditions: The Asymmetric Effect of Prosperity and Recession', *American Political Science Review* (1975).

BOLIN, OLOF, MEYERSON, PER-MARTIN, and STÅHL, INGEMAR, *Makten över maten: Livsmedelssektorns politiska ekonomi* (Stockholm: SNS, 1984).

BORCHERDING, THOMAS E., BUSH, WINSTON, C., and SPANN, ROBERT M., 'The Effects on Public Spending of the Divisibility of Public Outputs in Consumption, Bureaucratic Power, and the Size of the Tax-Sharing Group', in T. E. Borcherding (ed.), *Budgets and Bureaucrats: The Sources of Government Growth* (Durham, NC: Duke UP, 1977).

BORRE, OLE, 'Ideology and Class Voting in Denmark: A Preliminary Analysis', paper presented at the Joint Sessions of Workshops of the European Consortium for Political Research, Freiburg, 1983.

BOYNE, GEORGE A., 'Bureaucratic Power and Public Policies: A Test of the Rational Staff Maximization Hypothesis', *Political Studies* (1987).

BRETON, ALBERT, *The Economic Theory of Representative Government* (London and Basingstoke: Macmillan, 1974).

—— and WINTROBE, RONALD, 'The Equilibrium Size of a Budget-Maximizing Bureau: A Note on Niskanen's Theory of Bureaucracy', *Journal of Political Economy* (1975).

BRUIN, GERT P. de, 'Economic Theory of Bureaucracy and Public Good Allocation', in J.-E. Lane (ed.), *Bureaucracy and Public Choice*.

BUCHANAN, JAMES M., *The Limits of Liberty: Between Anarchy and Leviathan* (Chicago and London: Univ. of Chicago Press, 1975).

—— 'Political Equality and Private Property: The Distributional Paradox', in G. Dworkin, G. Bermant, and P. G. Brown (eds.), *Markets and Morals* (Washington and London: Hemisphere Publishing Corporation, 1977).

——*Market Failure and Government Failure*, Nobel Lecture, Uppsala, 12 December 1986.

—— and TULLOCK, GORDON, *The Calculus of Consent: Logical Foundations of Constitutional Democracy* (Ann Arbor, Mich.: Univ. of Michigan Press, 1969; 1st publ. in 1962).

BUSH, WINSTON C., and MACKAY, ROBERT J., 'Private Versus Public Sector Growth: A Collective Choice Approach', in T. E. Borcherding (ed.), *Budgets and Bureaucrats*.

BUTLER, DAVID, and STOKES, DONALD, *Political Change in Britain: The Evolution of Electoral Choice* (London and Basingstoke: Macmillan, 1974; 1st publ. in 1969).

CAMERON, DAVID R., 'The Expansion of the Public Economy: A Comparative Analysis', *American Political Science Review* (1978).

CAMPBELL, ANGUS, CONVERSE, PHILIP E., MILLER, WARREN E., and STOKES, DONALD E., *The American Voter* (New York: John Wiley & Sons, 1960).

—— GURIN, GERALD, and MILLER, WARREN E., *The Voter Decides* (Evanston, Ill., and White Plains, NY: Row Peterson & Co., 1954).

CHAPPELL, HENRY W., jun., and KEECH, WILLIAM R., 'A New View of Political Accountability for Economic Performance', *American Political Science Review* (1985).

CONOVER, PAMELA JOHNSTON, FELDMAN, STANLEY, and KNIGHT, KATHLEEN, 'Judging Inflation and Unemployment: The Origins of Retrospective Evaluations', *Journal of Politics* (1986).

CONVERSE, PHILIP E., 'Survey Research and the Decoding of Patterns in Ecological Data', in M. Dogan and S. Rokkan (eds.), *Quantitative Ecological Analysis in the Social Sciences* (Cambridge, Mass., and London: MIT Press, 1969).

CONYBEARE, JOHN A. C., 'Bureaucracy, Monopoly, and Competition: A Critical Analysis of the Budget-Maximizing Model of Bureaucracy', *American Journal of Political Science* (1984).

DAHL, ROBERT A., *Polyarchy: Participation and Opposition* (New Haven, Conn., and London: Yale UP, 1971).

DINKEL, REINER, 'Political Business Cycles in Germany and the United States: Some Theoretical and Empirical Considerations', in D. A. Hibbs, jun., H. Fassbinder, and R. D. Rivers (eds.), *Contemporary Political Economy: Studies of the Interdependence of Politics and Economics* (Amsterdam: North-Holland Publishing Company, 1981).

DOGAN, MATTEI (ed.), *The Mandarins of Western Europe: The Political Role of Top Civil Servants* (New York: John Wiley & Sons, 1975).

DOWNS, ANTHONY, *An Economic Theory of Democracy* (New York: Harper & Row, 1957).
—— *Inside Bureaucracy* (Boston: Little, Brown & Co., 1967).
DUNLEAVY, PATRICK, 'Bureaucrats, Budgets and the Growth of the State: Reconstructing an Instrumental Model', *British Journal of Political Science* (1985).
—— 'Explaining the Privatization Boom: Public Choice Versus Radical Approaches', *Public Administration* (1986).
DUNSIRE, ANDREW, 'Testing Theories: The Contribution of Bureaumetrics', in J.-E. Lane (ed.), *Bureaucracy and Public Choice.*
DWORKIN, RONALD, *Taking Rights Seriously* (Cambridge, Mass.: Harvard UP, 1977).
EHRENCRONA, OLOF, 'Politik, egoism och altruism', *Svenska Dagbladet*, 12 October 1986.
EHRENHEIM, JACOB VON, *Public Choice: En ny syn på svensk jordbrukspolitik* (Uppsala: Swedish Univ. of Agricultural Sciences, 1984).
ELSTER, JON, *Forklaring og dialektikk: Noen grunnbegreper i vitenskapsteorien* (Oslo: Pax, 1979).
—— *Ulysses and the Sirens: Studies in Rationality and Irrationality* (Cambridge etc.: Cambridge UP, 1979).
—— *Sour Grapes: Studies in the Subversion of Rationality* (Cambridge: Cambridge UP, 1983).
—— 'Rationality, Morality, and Collective Action', *Ethics* (1985).
—— *Rational Choice* (Oxford: Basil Blackwell, 1986).
FELDMAN, STANLEY, 'Economic Self-Interest and Political Behavior', *American Journal of Political Science* (1982).
—— 'Economic Self-Interest and the Vote: Evidence and Meaning', *Political Behavior* (1984).
FIORINA, MORRIS P., 'Economic Retrospective Voting in American National Elections: A Micro-Analysis', *American Journal of Political Science* (1978).
—— *Retrospective Voting in American National Elections* (New Haven, Conn.: Yale UP, 1981).
—— and NOLL, ROGER N., 'Voters, Bureaucrats and Legislators: A Rational Choice Perspective on the Growth of Bureaucracy', *Journal of Public Economics* (1978).
FISHEL, JEFF, Review article in the *American Political Science Review* (1979).
FLANAGAN, SCOTT C., 'Value Cleavages, Economic Cleavages, and the Japanese Voter', *American Journal of Political Science* (1980).
FREY, BRUNO S., 'Politico-Economic Models and Cycles', *Journal of Public Economics* (1978).
—— 'Politomerics of Government Behavior in a Democracy', *Scandinavian Journal of Economics* (1979).
—— and SCHNEIDER, FRIEDRICH, 'Politico-Economic Models in Competition

with Alternative Models: Which Predict Better?', *European Journal of Political Science* (1982).

FRIEDMAN, MILTON, 'The Methodology of Positive Economics', *Essays in Positive Economics* (Chicago: Univ. of Chicago Press, 1953).

GAUTHIER, DAVID, 'Reason and Maximization', in B. Barry and R. Hardin (eds.), *Rational Man and Irrational Society?*

GOODIN, ROBERT E., 'Possessive Individualism Again', *Political Studies* (1976).

—— 'Rational Politicians and Rational Bureaucrats in Washington and Whitehall', *Public Administration* (1982).

GOODMAN, SAUL, and KRAMER, GERALD H., 'Comment on Arcelus and Meltzer: The Effect of Aggregate Economic Conditions on Congressional Elections', *American Political Science Review* (1975).

GREENWOOD, ROYSTON, 'Bureaucracy: Servant or Master?' *Public Administration* (1974).

HADENIUS, AXEL, *A Crisis of the Welfare State? Opinions About Taxes and Public Expenditure in Sweden* (Stockholm: Almqvist & Wiksell International, 1986).

HAERPFER, CHRISTIAN, 'Value Change in Austria', unpubl. paper (Vienna: Institut für Konfliktforschung, 1987).

HAHN, FRANK, and HOLLIS, MARTIN (eds.), *Philosophy and Economic Theory* (Oxford: Oxford UP, 1979).

HAMMOND, PETER J., 'Utilitarianism, Uncertainty and Information', in Sen and Williams (eds.), *Utilitarianism and Beyond*.

HAPPY, J. R., 'Personal Experience and Government Responsibility for Economic Performance in Canadian Voting Behaviour', paper presented at the Annual Meeting of The American Political Science Association, Washington, 1984.

HARDIN, RUSSELL, *Collective Action* (Baltimore and London: The Johns Hopkins UP, 1982).

HARSANYI, JOHN C., *Essays on Ethics, Social Behavior, and Scientific Explanation* (Dordrecht and Boston: Reidel, 1976).

—— 'Morality and the Theory of Rational Behaviour', in Sen and Williams (eds.), *Utilitarianism and Beyond*.

HECKSCHER, GUNNAR, 'Konservatismen och utopierna', *Svenska Dagbladet*, 2 November 1986.

HECLO, HUGH, and WILDAVSKY, AARON, *The Private Government of Public Money* (London: Macmillan, 1974).

HERBERLE, RUDOLF, *From Democracy to Nazism: A Regional Case Study on Political Parties in Germany* (Baton Rouge: Louisiana State UP, 1945).

HERMANSSON, JÖRGEN, 'Rousseaus teori om allmänviljan', unpubl. paper, Department of Government, Univ. of Uppsala, 1987.

HIBBING, JOHN R., and ALFORD, JOHN R., 'The Electoral Impact of Economic Conditions: Who is Held Responsible?' *American Journal of Political Science* (1981).

HIBBS, DOUGLAS A., 'On the Demand for Economic Outcomes: Macroeconomic Performance and Mass Political Support in the United States, Great Britain, and Germany', *Journal of Politics* (1982).

HJERN, BENNY, 'Vad optimerar byråchefen?' *Statsvetenskaplig tidskrift* (1973).

HOLMBERG, SÖREN, *Svenska väljare* (Stockholm: Liber, 1981).

—— *Väljare i förändring* (Stockholm: Liber, 1984).

—— and GILLJAM, MIKAEL, *Väljare och val i Sverige* (Stockholm: Bonniers, 1987).

HOWARD, NIGEL, *Paradoxes of Rationality: Theory of Metagames and Political Behavior* (Cambridge, Mass.: MIT Press, 1971).

INGEMARSON, LARS, 'Public Choice och den offentliga sektorns tillväxt i den industrialiserade västvärlden', unpubl. paper, Department of Economics, Univ. of Lund, 1986.

IRWIN, GALEN A., ' "It All Depends on How You Look at It": Changes in Thinking About Politics and the Vote in the Netherlands', paper presented at the Joint Sessions of Workshops of the European Consortium for Political Research, Gothenburg, 1986.

JACKSON, P. M., *The Political Economy of Bureaucracy* (Oxford: Philip Allan, 1982).

JOHNSON, RONALD N., and LIBECAP, GARY D., 'Agency Growth and Bureaucratic Salaries', unpubl. paper, Montana State Univ. and Univ. of Arizona, June 1987.

JOHNSTON, RICHARD, *Public Opinion and Public Policy in Canada* (Toronto etc.: Univ. of Toronto Press, 1986).

JONUNG, LARS, 'Business Cycles and Political Changes in Sweden', *Skandinaviska Enskilda Banken Quarterly Review* (1985).

KALECKI, MICHAL, 'Political Aspects of Full Employment', *Political Quarterly* (1943).

KEY, V. O., jun., *The Responsible Electorate: Rationality in Presidential Voting 1936–1960* (Cambridge, Mass.: The Belknap Press of Harvard UP, 1966).

KIEWIET, D. RODERICK, *Macroeconomics and Micropolitics: The Electoral Effects of Economic Issues* (Chicago and London: Univ. of Chicago Press, 1983).

KINDER, DONALD R., and KIEWIET, D. RODERICK, 'Economic Discontent and Political Behavior: The Role of Personal Grievances and Collective Economic Judgments in Congressional Voting', *American Journal of Political Science* (1979).

—— 'Sociotropic Politics: The American Case', *British Journal of Political Science* (1981).

KRAMER, GERALD H., 'Short-Term Fluctuations in U.S. Voting Behavior, 1896–1964', *American Political Science Review* (1971).

—— 'The Ecological Fallacy Revisited: Aggregate- versus Individual-Level Findings on Economics and Elections, and Sociotropic Voting', *American Political Science Review* (1983).

KRISTENSEN, OLE P., 'The Logic of Political-Bureaucratic Decision-Making as a Cause of Governmental Growth', *European Journal of Political Research* (1980).

LANCASTER, THOMAS D., and LEWIS-BECK, MICHAEL S., 'The Spanish Voter: Tradition, Economics, Ideology', *Journal of Politics* (1986).

LANE, JAN-ERIK (ed.), *Bureaucracy and Public Choice* (London: Sage, 1987).

LAURIN, URBAN, *På heder och samvete: Skattefuskets orsaker och utbredning* (Stockholm: Norstedts, 1986).

LAZARSFELD, PAUL F., BERELSON, BERNARD, and GAUDET, HAZEL, *The People's Choice: How the Voter Makes up His Mind in a Presidential Campaign* (New York: Columbia UP, 1944).

LEWIN, LEIF, *Folket och eliterna: En studie i modern demokratisk teori* (Stockholm: Almqvist & Wiksell, 1970).

—— 'Utilitarianism and Rational Choice', *European Journal of Political Research* (1988).

—— JANSSON, BO, and SÖRBOM, DAG, *The Swedish Electorate 1887–1968* (Stockholm: Almqvist & Wiksell, 1972).

LEWIS-BECK, MICHAEL S., 'Economic Conditions and Executive Popularity: The French Experience', *American Journal of Political Science* (1980).

—— 'Economics and the French Voter: A Microanalysis', *Public Opinion Quarterly* (1983).

—— 'Economics and Electoral Behavior in France', in N. J. Vig and S. E. Schier (eds.), *Political Economy in Western Democracies* (London: Holmes and Meier, 1985).

—— 'Comparative Economic Voting: Britain, France, Germany, Italy', *American Journal of Political Science* (1986).

—— and EULAU, HEINZ, 'Introduction: Economic Conditions and Electoral Behavior in Transnational Perspective', in H. Eulau and M. S. Lewis-Beck (eds.), *Economic Conditions and Electoral Outcomes: The United States and Western Europe* (New York: Agathon Press, 1985).

LIPPMANN, WALTER, *The Public Philosophy* (London: Hamish Hamilton, 1955).

LISTHAUG, OLA, and MILLER, ARTHUR H., 'Public Support for Tax Evasion: Self-Interest or Symbolic Politics?' *European Journal of Political Research* (1985).

LOCKSLEY, GARETH, 'The Political Business Cycles: Alternative Interpretations', in P. Whiteley (ed.), *Models of Political Economy*.

LYBECK, JOHAN A., 'Finns det en politisk konjunkturcykel i Sverige?' *Ekonomisk debatt* (1983).

LYBECK, JOHAN A., 'A Simultaneous Model of Politico-Economic Interaction in Sweden, 1970–82, *European Journal of Political Research* (1985).
—— *The Growth of Government in Developed Countries* (Aldershot: Gower, 1986).
LÄCHLER, ULRICH, 'The Political Business Cycle under Rational Voting Behavior', *Public Choice* (1984).
MACRAE, C. DUNCAN, 'A Political Model of the Business Cycle', *Journal of Political Economy* (1977).
MADSEN, HENRIK J., 'Electoral Outcomes and Macro-Economic Policies: The Scandinavian Cases', in P. Whiteley (ed.), *Models of Political Economy*.
MARCH, JAMES G., and OLSEN, JOHAN P., 'The New Institutionalism: Organizational Factors in Political Life', *American Political Science Review* (1984).
MARGOLIS, HOWARD, 'A New Model of Rational Choice', *Ethics* (1981), 265–79.
—— *Selfishness, Altruism, and Rationality* (Cambridge: Cambridge UP, 1982).
MARGOLIS, JULIUS, 'Comment', *Journal of Law and Economics* (1975).
MARKUS, GREGORY B., 'The Impact of Personal and National Economic Conditions on the Presidential Vote: A Pooled Cross-Sectional Analysis', unpubl. paper, March 1986.
MCCALLUM, BENNETT T., 'The Political Business Cycle: An Empirical Test', *Southern Economic Journal* (1977).
MEEHL, PAUL E., 'The Selfish Voter Paradox and the Thrown-Away Vote Argument', *American Political Science Review* (1977).
MEIER, KENNETH J., *Regulation: Politics, Bureaucracy, and Economics* (New York: St Martin's Press, 1985).
MELLBOURN, ANDERS, *Byråkratins ansikten: Rolluppfattningar hos svenska högre statstjänstemän* (Stockholm: Liber, 1979).
MERRIAM, CHARLES, and GOSNELL, HAROLD F., *Non-Voting: Causes and Methods of Control* (Chicago: Univ. of Chicago Press, 1924).
MERTON, ROBERT K., *Social Theory and Social Structure* (rev. edn., New York: Free Press, 1957).
MILLER, ARTHUR H., and LISTHAUG, OLA, 'Economic Effects on the Vote in Norway', *Political Behavior* (1984).
MILLER, DAVID, *Philosophy and Ideology in Hume's Political Thought* (Oxford: Clarendon Press, 1981).
MILLER, GARY J., and MOE, TERRY M., 'Bureaucrats, Legislators, and the Size of Government', *American Political Science Review* (1983).
MINFORD, PATRICK, and PEEL, DAVID, 'The Political Theory of the Business Cycle', *European Economic Review* (1982).
MIRRLEES, J. A., 'The Economic Uses of Utilitarianism', in A. Sen and B. Williams (eds.), *Utilitarianism and Beyond* (Cambridge: Cambridge UP, 1982).

MITCHELL, WILLIAM C., 'Efficiency, Responsibility, and Democratic Politics', in J. R. Pennock and J. W. Chapman (eds.), *Nomos XXV: Liberal Democracy* (New York and London: New York UP, 1983).

MONROE, KRISTEN R., 'Econometric Analyses of Electoral Behavior: A Critical Review', *Political Behavior* (1979).

—— and ERICKSON, LYNDA, 'The Economy and Political Support: The Canadian Case', *Journal of Politics* (1986).

MUELLER, DENNIS C., *Public Choice* (Cambridge etc.: Cambridge UP, 1979).

NADEL, MARK V., and ROURKE, FRANCIS E., 'Bureaucracies', in F. I. Greenstein and N. W. Polsby (eds.), *Governmental Institutions and Processes: Handbook of Political Science*, v (Reading: Addison-Wesley, 1975).

NAGEL, ERNEST, 'Assumptions in Economic Theory', in A. Ryan (ed.), *The Philosophy of Social Explanation* (Oxford: Oxford UP, 1973).

NISKANEN, WILLIAM A., *Bureaucracy and Representative Government* (Chicago and New York: Aldine-Atherton, 1971).

—— 'Bureaucrats and Politicians', *Journal of Law and Economics* (1975).

NORDHAUS, WILLIAM D., 'The Political Business Cycle', *Review of Economic Studies* (1975).

OPPENHEIM, FELIX E., 'Self-Interest and Public Interest', *Political Concepts: A Reconstruction* (Oxford: Basil Blackwell, 1981).

OBERNDÖRFER, DIETER, RATTINGER, HANS, and SCHMITT, KARL (eds.), *Wirtschaftlicher Wandel, religiöser Wandel und Wertwandel: Folgen für das politische Verhalten in der Bundesrepublik Deutschland* (Ordo Politicus, 25; Berlin: Duncker & Humblot, 1985).

ORZECHOWSKI, WILLIAM, 'Economic Models of Bureaucracy: Survey, Extensions, and Evidence', in T. E. Borcherding (ed.), *Budgets and Bureaucrats: The Sources of Government Growth* (Durham, NC: Duke UP, 1977).

OSTROM, ELINOR, 'Multiorganizational Arrangements and Coordination: An Application of Institutional Analysis', in F.-X. Kaufmann, G. Majone, and V. Ostrom (eds.), *Guidance, Control, and Evaluation in the Public Sector* (Berlin and New York: de Gruyter, 1985).

OWENS, JOHN R., and OLSON, EDWARD C., 'Economic Fluctuations and Congressional Elections', *American Journal of Political Science* (1980).

OYE, KENNETH A., 'Explaining Cooperation Under Anarchy: Hypotheses and Strategies', *World Politics* (1985).

PALDAM, MARTIN, 'Is There an Electional Cycle? A Comparative Study of National Accounts', *Scandinavian Journal of Economics* (1979).

—— 'An Essay on the Rationality of Economic Policy: The Test-Case of the Electional Cycle', *Public Choice* (1981).

PARFIT, DEREK, *Reasons and Persons* (Oxford: Clarendon Press, 1984).

PENNOCK, J. ROLAND, 'The One and the Many: A Note on the Concept', in C. J. Friedrich (ed.), *Nomos V: The Public Interest* (New York: Atherton Press, 1962).

PETERSSON, OLOF, *Väljarna och världspolitiken* (Stockholm: Norstedts, 1982).

POPPER, KARL R., *Conjectures and Refutations: The Growth of Scientific Knowledge* (London: Routledge & Kegan Paul, 1972; 1st publ. in 1963).

PRZEWORSKI, ADAM and SPRAGUE, JOHN, *Paper Stones: A History of Electoral Socialism* (Chicago and London: Univ. of Chicago Press, 1986).

PUTNAM, ROBERT D., 'The Political Attitudes of Senior Civil Servants in Western Europe: A Preliminary Report', *British Journal of Political Science* (1973).

RAPOPORT, ANATOL, 'Prisoner's Dilemma. Recollections and Observations', in B. Barry and R. Hardin (eds.), *Rational Man and Irrational Society? An Introduction and Sourcebook* (Beverly Hills: Sage, 1982).

—— and CHAMMAH, ALBERT M., *Prisoner's Dilemma* (Ann Arbor, Mich.: Univ. of Michigan Press, 1965).

RATTINGER, HANS, 'Collective and Individual Economic Judgments and Voting in West Germany, 1961–1984', *European Journal of Political Research* (1986).

REED, STEVEN, and BRUNK, GREGORY G., 'A Test of Two Theories of Economically Motivated Voting: The Case of Japan', *Comparative Politics* (1984).

RICE, STUART A., *Quantitative Aspects of Politics* (New York: Alfred A. Knopf, 1928).

RIKER, WILLIAM H., *Liberalism Against Populism: A Confrontation Between the Theory of Democracy and the Theory of Social Choice* (San Francisco: W. H. Freeman and Co., 1982).

—— and ORDESHOOK, PETER C., *An Introduction to Positive Political Theory* (Englewood Cliffs, NJ: Prentice-Hall, 1973).

RIVERS, DOUGLAS, 'Microeconomics and Macroeconomics: A Solution to the Kramer Problem', unpubl. paper, March 1986.

ROBINSON, W. S., 'Ecological Correlations and the Behavior of Individuals', *American Sociological Review* (1950).

ROSE, RICHARD, *Understanding Big Government: The Programme Approach* (London: Sage, 1984).

ROTHSTEIN, BO, 'Litteraturgranskningar', *Statsvetenskaplig tidskrift* (1988).

ROWLEY, CHARLES K., TOLLISON, ROBERT D., and TULLOCK, GORDON (eds.), *The Political Economy of Rent-Seeking* (Boston: Kluwer Academic Publ., 1988).

SAMUELSSON, KURT, 'Den spräckliga högern', *Svenska Dagbladet*, 9 November 1986.

SCHLOZMAN, KAY LEHMAN, and VERBA, SIDNEY, *Injury to Insult: Unemployment, Class, and Political Response* (Cambridge, Mass. and London: Harvard UP, 1979).

SCHUBERT, GLENDON, 'Is There a Public Interest Theory?', in C. J. Friedrich (ed.), *Nomos V: The Public Interest* (New York: Atherton Press, 1962).

SEARS, DAVID O., HENSLER, CARL P., and SPEER, LESLIE K., 'Whites' Opposition to "Busing": Self-Interest or Symbolic Politics?' *American Political Science Review* (1979).

—— LAU, RICHARD R., TYLER, TOM R., and HARRIS, M. ALLEN, jun., 'Self-Interest vs. Symbolic Politics in Policy Attitudes and Presidential Voting', *American Political Science Review* (1980).

—— and LAU, RICHARD R., 'Inducing Apparently Self-Interested Political Preferences', *American Journal of Political Science* (1983).

SELF, PETER, *Political Theories of Modern Government* (London: George Allen & Unwin, 1985).

SEN, AMARTYA, 'Isolation, Assurance and the Social Rate of Discount', *Quarterly Journal of Economics* (1967).

—— (ed.), *Choice, Welfare and Measurement* (Oxford: Basil Blackwell, 1982).

—— 'Behaviour and the Concept of Preference' in Sen (ed.), *Choice, Welfare and Measurement*.

—— 'Rational Fools', in Sen (ed.), *Choice, Welfare and Measurement*.

—— and WILLIAMS, BERNARD (eds.), *Utilitarianism and Beyond* (Cambridge: Cambridge UP, 1982).

SIEGFRIED, ANDRÉ, *Tableau politique de la France de l'Ouest sous la Troisième République* (Paris: Colin, 1913).

SIGELMAN, LEE, and TSAI, YUNG-MEI, 'Personal Finances and Voting Behavior: A Reanalysis', *American Politics Quarterly* (1981).

SPANN, ROBERT M., 'Public Versus Private Provision of Governmental Services', in T. E. Borcherding (ed.), *Budgets and Bureaucrats: The Sources of Government Growth* (Durham, NC: Duke UP, 1977).

STAAF, ROBERT J., 'The Growth of the Educational Bureaucracy: Do Teachers Make a Difference?', in T. E. Borcherding (ed.), *Budgets and Bureaucrats: The Sources of Government Growth* (Durham, NC: Duke UP, 1977).

STIGLER, GEORGE J., 'General Economic Conditions and National Elections', *American Economic Review* (1973).

SØRENSEN, RUNE J., 'Bureaucratic Decision-Making and the Growth of Public Expenditure', in J.-E. Lane (ed.), *Bureaucracy and Public Choice*.

TARSCHYS, DANIEL, 'The Growth of Public Expenditures: Nine Modes of Explanation', *Scandinavian Political Studies* (1975).

TEN, C. L., *Mill on Liberty* (Oxford: Clarendon Press, 1980).

THOENIG, JEAN CLAUDE, and FRIEDBERG, ERHARD, 'The Power of the Field Staff: The Case of the Ministry of Public Works, Urban Affairs and Housing in France', in A. F. Leemans (ed.), *The Management of Change in Government* (The Hague: Martinus Nijhoff, 1976).

TINGSTEN, HERBERT, *Political Behavior: Studies in Election Statistics* (London: P. S. King & Son, 1937).

TUFTE, EDWARD R., 'Determinants of the Outcomes of Mid-term Congressional Elections', *American Political Science Review* (1975).

TUFTE, EDWARD R., *Political Control of the Economy* (Princeton, NJ: Princeton UP, 1978).

TULLOCK, GORDON, *The Politics of Bureaucracy* (Washington, DC: Public Affairs Press, 1965).

USHER, DAN, *The Economic Prerequisite to Democracy* (Oxford: Basil Blackwell, 1981).

WEALE, ALBERT, *Political Theory and Social Policy* (London: Macmillan, 1983).

WEATHERFORD, M. STEPHEN, 'Economic Conditions and Electoral Outcomes: Class Differences in the Political Response to Recession', *American Journal of Political Science* (1978).

—— 'Economic Voting and the "Symbolic Politics" Argument: A Reinterpretation and Synthesis', *American Political Science Review* (1983).

WHITELEY, PAUL (ed.), *Models of Political Economy* (London and Beverly Hills: Sage, 1980).

—— *Political Control of the Macroeconomy: The Political Economy of Public Policy Making* (London: Sage, 1986).

WIDES, JEFFREY W., 'Self-Perceived Economic Change and Political Orientations: A Preliminary Exploration', *American Politics Quarterly* (1976).

—— 'Perceived Economic Competency and the Ford/Carter Election', *Public Opinion Quarterly* (1979).

WILCOX, WILLIAM H., 'Egoists, Consequentialists, and Their Friends', *Philosophy and Public Affairs* (1987).

WILDAVSKY, AARON, *The Politics of the Budgetary Process* (Boston: Little, Brown & Co., 1964).

WITTMAN, DONALD, 'Parties as Utility Maximizers', *American Political Science Review* (1973).

—— 'Candidate Motivation: A Synthesis of Alternative Theories', *American Political Science Review* (1983).

WOLF, CHARLES, jun., 'A Theory of Nonmarket Failure: Framework for Implementation Analysis', *Journal of Law and Economics* (1979).

Index